I0760146

A History Of Punk

A History Of Punk

Punk & Pistolry

Stephen Palmer

WHITE OWL
AN IMPRINT OF PEN & SWORD BOOKS LTD.
YORKSHIRE – PHILADELPHIA

First published in Great Britain in 2025 by
White Owl
An imprint of Pen & Sword Books Limited
Yorkshire – Philadelphia

ISBN 978 1 03612 030 6

A CIP catalogue record for this book is available from the British Library.

Typeset by Mac Style
Printed in the UK by CPI Group (UK) Ltd, Croydon, CR0 4YY.

The Publisher's authorised representative in the EU for product safety is Authorised Rep Compliance Ltd., Ground Floor, 71 Lower Baggot Street, Dublin D02 P593, Ireland.
www.arccompliance.com

For a complete list of Pen & Sword titles please contact

PEN & SWORD BOOKS LIMITED
47 Church Street, Barnsley, South Yorkshire, S70 2AS, England
E-mail: enquiries@pen-and-sword.co.uk
Website: www.pen-and-sword.co.uk
or
PEN AND SWORD BOOKS
1950 Lawrence Road, Havertown, PA 19083, USA
E-mail: uspen-and-sword@casematepublishers.com
Website: www.penandswordbooks.com

This book is dedicated to the memory of Dave Greenfield.

For
Andrew & Susan.

Contents

Acknowledgements

With thanks to: Anthony Clark, Jon Courtenay Grimwood, Ian Dickson, Hank Hansford, Steve Hardy, Hal Harries, Jon High, Andrew Johns, Lynn Lee, Kenneth O'Brien, Icarus Peel, Tom Ryder Runton, Bill Sewell, Kevin Shepherd, Aidan @ Tubeway Records, and Neal Vaughan. Thanks also to everyone at Unofficial Damned Nonsense at Facebook who assisted me.

Special thanks to: Marc Burrows, Susan Carrington & Andrew Czezowski, Mélanie Dangereuse de Clegane, Simon Draper, John "Eddie" Edwards, Lora Logic, Alan Lee Shaw and Jon Webster.

I would like to thank Jonathan Wright and Charlotte Mitchell at Pen & Sword Books.

Introduction

One day in 1977, when I was fifteen, I walked past the transistor radio in the kitchen of my parents' house and heard an extraordinary sound. It was a rock song, but one like nothing I'd ever heard before. Transfixed, I halted, listening to the music until it faded and the DJ spoke. He said it was *5 Minutes* by The Stranglers.

From that moment I was a fan – of The Stranglers, of exciting new music, of a genre that I soon learned was called punk rock. That same year I had discovered Genesis, Yes, and above all Tangerine Dream, whom I loved, and still do; ditto for the two prog rock behemoths. But I also loved The Stranglers, and The Damned. Music entered my life that year, and in the most dramatic style. What struck me about *5 Minutes* – a psychological force akin to running into a brick wall – was the keyboard sound and the sheer visceral energy of the song. It was utterly compelling. It was incredible! It was mesmerising, and I wanted more.

By now, via friends at school who were also enamoured with the punk explosion, and from reading and watching television news reports, I knew of the Sex Pistols and the bands around them. Though the Pistols weren't on *Top Of The Pops,* I saw photographs of them in the music press; and these images made me hesitate. Something raw and dangerous emanated from those four young men, and I, shy and a bit of a misfit, felt a touch of fear. It was difficult to feel afraid of The Damned, chaotic and ebullient though they were, but the Sex Pistols somehow beamed terror rays outward into staid society circles, mostly through the intense gaze of Johnny Rotten.

Punk was something that had never been seen before in Britain, a very un-British movement, in fact, which directly challenged the establishment and everything it stood for rather than doffing its cap. That came as a shock to me. I'd never heard the term 'establishment' before, and we hadn't covered it with Miss Picken in history lessons. The core song of the movement, *Anarchy In The U.K.*, mentioned the I.R.A., the M.P.L.A. and the U.D.A., all terror organisations bombing in Northern Ireland and the British mainland. That was no joke. Dozens of people were being killed. That a punk song referenced those organisations was truly shocking, and even I, naïve and fairly clueless about society, grasped the significance and possible consequences.

But because I was a couple of years too young to get involved myself, and because at the time I didn't play any musical instruments or have the confidence to go out and do anything, I followed my passion for music by simply *listening*. All forms of music attracted me in those formative years of my life: The Stranglers and The Damned, Tangerine Dream, Yes, Pink Floyd and Genesis, and then other, *stranger* music introduced by accident after listening to Radio 1 and Radio 3: Steve Reich, Terry Riley and Karlheinz Stockhausen amongst others. I also liked pop music: The Sweet and T Rex. I began listening to Annie Nightingale's Sunday show, where I heard the Floyd's *Animals* for the first time and discovered the hypnotic music of Jean-Michel Jarre.

In fact, it was the mesmeric in music which most captivated me at the time. Steve Reich entranced me, Tangerine Dream took me across sonic oceans, Jean-Michel Jarre hypnotised me. But Dave Greenfield of The Stranglers was a musician I always returned to, time after time, year after year. As Hugh Cornwell wrote when Greenfield died of complications following Covid-19, their keyboard wizard was the difference between The Stranglers and all the other new bands of the era. But Greenfield was one man of four. The Stranglers were one of those groups, like Yes, whose whole was more than the sum of its parts. As a young, impressionable person, I sensed that without realising why. I *knew* what I liked. I felt that mysterious, incessant, unavoidable tug of something special, something that grabbed my emotions, that was a thrill, a surprise. Many of the punk bands, especially when the first phase of the movement was over and it morphed into post-punk and New Wave, began appearing on *Top Of The Pops*, allowing me to get a handle on the range and variety of music available. They were such exciting times. So much great music appeared in the late seventies, so many classic albums.

I loved music then. I still do. I play various instruments, had my own underground band for a quarter of a century, record and play live, and I'm always on the hunt for new music and novel groups. That's why I wrote this book. Music is a metaphor for the emotional side of the human condition. I live that side out in various forms. That I keep rediscovering the music of my own past, remembering the thrill, feeling the excitement and wonder, is of high significance to me. This book is an exploration and a memento.

Chapter 1

Exploding In Britain

It was filthy and it was furious. But it was so much more. It was class agitation, and in some cases class war. It was a kind of anarchist philosophy. It was the rage of urban boredom in grey tower blocks. It was an early consequence of a new wave of feminists. It was excitement, exultation, the exploitation of random chance. It was attitude. And it was music – exultant music, full of anger that had not been seen before. In 1976 only nine years separated the tumultuous speed-riffing and breathless vocals of The Damned's debut single *New Rose* from the elegant, mannered, psychedelic tunesmithery of *Sergeant Pepper's Lonely Hearts Club Band.* So, it was filthy and furious, and often chaotic, but it still managed to upturn the received wisdom of those nine years, to the surprise of every single onlooker.

Ironically, given the intensity of punk's British explosion in 1976, the music term originated in America a few years earlier, when various critics began referring to the music of bands such as MC5 and Iggy and the Stooges as punk rock. 'Punk', in America, was a term with various meanings, but in particular it meant a low man, a worthless youth – a novice, a newbie. This word had been used in American music circles with increasing range and mockery from as far back as 1970. Various garage bands from the later sixties and early seventies, all tough-guy leather jackets and misunderstood attitude, were making stripped down music based on the drums/bass/guitar/singer template. They were the punks, and their jagged, rough-around-the-edges, anti-psychedelic songs were termed punk rock. Another band enamoured with this garage scene was The Ramones, who would go on to have a vital role in the lighting of punk's British blue touch paper in 1976.

Punk was an all-encompassing scene. It had furious music that hit its youthful fans between the eyes with the force of a lobbed amp head – three chords and the truth in less than three minutes. It had its own characteristic dance: pogoing. It had plenty of the adolescent lack of hygiene in its craze for spitting at gigs. It even had a philosophy of sorts: reject, reject, reject. A large part of punk was about moving away from the past, notably from Britain's often twee music heritage, not to mention the expanded musical suites of prog rock; but at the same time it embraced radical energy, furious ranting, and a D.I.Y. attitude that was also about turning away from corporate bodies such as record labels and publishers. There was a nihilistic extreme, but there was relevant stuff too: *God save the Queen… a fascist regime.* In 1977, the year of Queen Elizabeth II's silver jubilee, that was about as shocking a public statement as could be made in cosy, pipe-and-slippers, traditional Britain.

And it had fashion statements – glorious, iconic, ironic fashion statements, from red tartan to the safety pin, from cut and torn paper artwork to metal chain collars. No punk walking down a British high street in 1976 could possibly be overlooked; and that was, in part, the point. Hair was no longer left mousey, or brown, or weak tea yellow, it was dyed a range of dayglo colours. Moreover, that hair was not left to waft about in the chill English breeze. It was treated with harsh products and whipped up into spikes and mohicans, making every tall lad in leathers and boots appear threatening to the bowler-hatted normals trudging from workplace to railway station. Television news programmes ran stories on punks, the general stance being: who are these human aliens from the suburbs? The British had been part charmed, part amused by hippies and the rise of psychedelia, which although radical at its inception, soon became limp, if still colourful. Yet at least psychedelia was in general whimsical and self-referentially English. Punk was dangerous because anger, to the British, is dangerous. As one of punk's Great Enemies Pink Floyd put it: *Quiet desperation is the English way.* But there was nothing quiet about punk. It was full of rage and it did not care who knew that.

Punk, though, despite this multimedia assault on a stunned nation, was at heart one of a series of scenes rooted in the British genius for music. Yes, rock 'n' roll started in America. Yes, the garage scene began in America. Yes, the Summer of Love had its heart in San Francisco. Brits took those scenes and gave them their own spin – superbly, in the case of psychedelia. By the seventies, having passed Beatlemania to the rest of the world, Britain was exporting Led Zeppelin, prog rock, art rock, and much, much more.

MC5 and The Ramones were pretty neat, but America had nothing like the Sex Pistols, The Damned, The Clash or The Stranglers. Partly that was an accident of scale, for the British scenes were usually formed from small, local, beating hearts of dissent; and as Britain had one fifth the population of America and a fraction of its land mass, Brits did local brilliantly. Their music came from unique minds: youthful, artistic, observant, working on a small scale. Young British songwriters took their personal experiences of life and used a national genius for songwriting to create enduring anthems. Not all of them were anthemic in the melodic sense, though some of them were great tunes. Punk rock was a thrash, and as often as not those thrashes were three chord diatribes with little discernible melody. Nothing wrong with that, of course. *God Save The Queen,* once heard, is impossible to forget.

This music too was a kind of Year Zero, determined not to reference the past, to start pretty much from scratch in fact, and that meant no keyboards, and certainly no synthesizers. When those masters of melody The Stranglers became entangled with the punk scene they were ostracised, partly because of their moustachioed keyboards player Dave Greenfield – who could play *fast* – and because they could write great tunes that crept into listeners' heads like sweat-stained earworms. Besides, there was a rumour that Greenfield liked Hawkwind, and that was forbidden. In musical style, in splenetic songs, in thrash and burn, punk kicked out the past and ushered in a new age of anger, rabid with fury, the spiky hairdo its totem, its goal to bring anarchy, if not the extreme of nihilism itself, to the masses.

Anger is an emotion, and human beings feel emotions for a very good reason. We have evolved this way over hundreds of thousands of years. Emotions are critical to our existence as sane individuals. They are our way of understanding human values. We can grasp that while a dead apple tree leaf is of no value, except to fungi, the apples that grow from those trees are quite important to us because they are a source of nourishment. Meanwhile, our friends and family are of critical importance, creating the social webs in which we live. In order to express the relative value of these parts of our lives to ourselves and to those around us, emotions evolved, all of them with physical components, that the messages contained in emotion would be impossible to miss. Thus, the message of grief is loss – the loss of a sibling, of a dear friend. We weep. The message of shame is moral ostracism, while the message of fear is danger.

The critical messages contained in anger are all about frustration: personal frustration most often, but also frustration about the life situations of others, and frustration at the slings and arrows of outrageous fortune, when life itself seems to be placing obstacles all around us. Frustration occurs when we face obstacles, and when we need to express how we feel about such obstacles, we get angry. Life without anger would be impossible. We *need* to tell ourselves that because we have dynamic minds, updating constantly, and we need to tell others about these feelings because they are our support system and our psychological mirrors.

For punks, anger was rooted in the frustrations of urban living, of a class system that favoured the landed rich and the sons of Eton, of wealth inequality, of a poverty of political representation, and most of all of grey, antiseptic tedium. Buzzcocks had a song called *Boredom* on their iconic *Spiral Scratch EP,* one of the earliest punk releases, which spoke of being hedged in and frustrated: *Now there's nothing behind me, and I'm already a has-been.* Its brilliant minimalism included a guitar anti-solo: essentially a couple of notes, repeated. But this was the real deal. Howard Devoto and Pete Shelley, both from Bolton, felt energised by the nascent punk scene, which offered them something novel, exciting, and filled with possibilities.

In his song *Rise,* John Lydon expressed the opinion ten years later, when even post-punk was heading into the cultural rear view mirror, that *anger is an energy.* And it is. Anger in the mid-1970s was a potent psychological fuel for frustrated urban youth. Britain had long been a hidebound nation, and British kids knew that – on dirty streets, in suburban blandness, inside hovels of light industry, and even at school and college, both of which were based on the factory educational model of the nineteenth century. It was the anger generated by frustration that stopped their minds turning beige. Just as hippies had changed a black and white world into one of rainbow colour, they were going to turn their bland British world dayglo.

Of course, the British are good at irony, so even the most callow of the nation's youth grasped the possibilities for satire and self-referential mockery as well as for wrathful self-expression in punk. After all, Buzzcocks' *Boredom* pointed a waspish finger at the perceived limitations of the punk scene itself. Punk had attitude, but it was not all about attitude.

British creative individuals tend to have an understanding of the subtle art of not standing out. Yet punk was different. Most punks were just too energised to consider self-reference. Their music was an unsubtle outburst. Though punk did have a philosophy – do it yourself, don't trust the record companies, reject the past, embrace your own scene – its existential anger did not in the early days allow for much intellectual speculation. That was left to the brainy bands of post-punk, who not only knew what nuance was but knew how to utilise it.

Punk music was a sonic explosion. It deafened and it burned. Its drug of preference was already inside adolescent bodies, conveniently provided by nature: adrenaline.

The music press, meanwhile, sensed that something was up as the scene began to appear. In those days, when kids bought printed magazines, and newspaper circulations were measured in the tens of millions, there were four main music mags: *New Musical Express,* better known as *NME, Sounds, Melody Maker* and *Record Mirror.* A classic *NME* front cover of 1977 featured The Clash, while an October 1976 cover featured the Sex Pistols (for whom *NME* journalist Nick Kent played occasional guitar). Buzzcocks were also the stars in 1977. Adverts were full of punk, spelled out in asymmetric cut-up print, the ink wiping off to stain readers' fingers. The Anarchy In The U.K. Tour received a full-page advert, featuring the Sex Pistols, The Damned and The Clash… oh, and Johnny Thunder's Heartbreakers from America. The Damned's *New Rose* and the Sex Pistols' *Anarchy In The U.K.* were both advertised as singles available to buy. This was new. This was different. This was not prog.

British radio was quicker off the mark than its often cringeworthy televisual cousin. In the main that was because of one man – John Peel. Peel *loved* music. Being a disc jockey and becoming a media personality like so many of his coiffured colleagues was not of interest to him, except, in the first case, in that it allowed him to broadcast extraordinary new music to the masses via his Radio 1 show. Peel was a vital mode of publicity to many punk bands. Yet for all that he bestrode the punk scene as a radio colossus, Annie Nightingale, another true music lover, also grasped the energy and importance of punk. Best known at the time for her Sunday progressive show, when she took over BBC television's *Old Grey Whistle Test* from Bob Harris in 1978, she quickly began championing new bands. She wanted to listen to the sounds of the musical underground, then nurture them by giving them exposure. And so, slowly, via sounds and visuals, and some months after the explosion had ripped through British culture, the mass media started to understand the significance of the new development.

By then, however, it was pretty much too late.

Like the time around the Summer of Love in 1967, a time which according to psychedelic purists lasted far less than a year, the Summer of Hate a decade later was brief and to the point. An explosion, after all, is already long over when your ears stop ringing and the glare in your eyes fades away. Thus it was with punk in Britain. 1976 was the year it was born, 1977 was the year it lived, 1978 was the year people began talking about post-punk. Arguably the first post-punk album, *Black & White* by The Stranglers, was released in May 1978. Some say the name Sex Pistols had not even been formalised just two and a half years earlier, when those nascent punks gigged in London.

Punk, then, was a cultural explosion. It tore through traditional British culture at all levels – musical, social, political. Music was forever transformed by it, society was riven, ripped and perturbed, and politics, which had for centuries been the preserve of entitled men from posh schools, was alarmed by it. The hippies of the previous decade had espoused political intent, and even had some success, not least when it came to changing public perception of the Vietnam conflict and America's role in global affairs. Punk also had a political agenda, but it was not just going to protest on British streets. It wanted to transform society. Punks hated the Tories, but they often hated Labour too, some of them even against the left wing of the party supposed to be on their side. The tide was set for anarchy in the U.K., something which would be broadcast through the vehicle of song.

Chapter 2

Tales From Progressive Groups

But what music exactly was it that the punk movement rejected? It was *prog* – progressive rock.

1967 was a watershed in British and American music because of the Summer of Love and psychedelia, a musical form rooted in novel influences, notably from India, but also in the general move in various media away from black and white into colour. Psychedelia also had its own drug: LSD. Magic mushrooms, peyote and DMT were groovy too.

In Britain, psychedelia was a movement based in London. Naturally, the Beatles, bestriding the Western world's popular music, were there at its inception, but so too were a band soon to take over their preeminent position – Pink Floyd. The two bands even shared Abbey Road recording studios. But for the Beatles, reacting to the hell of touring on the road in 1966, 1967 was about expanding the vinyl single format into something never seen before. They wanted to make *albums,* serious albums, albums that took months and months to record, in painstaking detail, using novel technology, and under the sway of grass and acid. Paul McCartney was being influenced by classical and avant garde music, George Harrison had discovered the sitar, while John Lennon was reading newspapers and circus posters to glean lyrics; and growing his hair. One of psychedelia's defining characteristics was its whimsy, matching the eccentricity of the British national character, a whimsy beautifully expressed by Pink Floyd's presiding guru Syd Barrett. But psychedelia was over by 1968, when a darker, rougher, more rock 'n' roll feel emerged. 1969 was worse – really dark, especially in America.

Progressive rock music and the LP format had some of their roots in all this. One of the earliest prog albums was King Crimson's extraordinary *In The Court Of The Crimson King*, from 1969. As the sixties gave way to the seventies, progressive rock acquired the characteristics which marked it out:

an almost academic approach to music, a willingness to explore classical and other influences, an emphasis on technical skill when playing, and, to match the move from single to LP, a move from three-minute pop songs to twenty-minute epics. Lyrically, prog had moved on from love and teenage tragedy to loftier concerns. By the end of the first half of the seventies all the beloved classic prog albums had been released: *The Dark Side Of The Moon, Close To The Edge, Selling England By The Pound, Larks' Tongues In Aspic.* These LPs were like sonic monoliths – global smashes, firm favourites of innumerable (usually male) devotees, and, in the case of Pink Floyd's masterpiece, simply inescapable. But by the middle of the decade the self-regarding, casually arrogant, puffed-up side of prog began to emerge.

Even fans were a little taken aback by the soggy middle of *Tales From Topographic Oceans* by Yes – a double album of two or three good sides. Emerson, Lake & Palmer meanwhile, with their massive touring lorries and highbrow classical references, encapsulated the bloated, pretentious aspect of the genre. Prog was in danger of disappearing up its own backside. There was also a hippie wing of the movement, led by bands such as Gong, signed up by Richard Branson's Virgin Records, then only just beginning its remarkable run. The whole scene was beginning to smell off.

One of Virgin Records' most interesting signings was the Sex Pistols, fronted by one of rock music's greatest characters: John Lydon, or as he was renamed, Johnny Rotten. Although Lydon these days cannot recall where he got the infamous item of clothing – possibly nicked from a street stall, as he put it years afterwards – his Pink Floyd T shirt with the words *I HATE* scrawled above the quartet's heads became one of punk's iconic images. It was a D.I.Y. attack on the rock establishment that perfectly summed up the zeitgeist. Not only were Pink Floyd good at playing their instruments, they hobnobbed with the best engineers, were fabulously wealthy, and could indulge in hobbies such as collecting cars. Pink Floyd became the band that punks loved to hate – a veritable bandwagon of contempt. Yet even that outrage was somewhat manufactured, since the prevailing attitude of the time, to Lydon and others, was actually not quite so black and white. As Lydon revealed in later interviews, he liked *The Dark Side Of The Moon.* David Gilmour in turn, when asked about the Sex Pistols, replied in that soft, cultivated accent of his that he thought they were rather good.

The hatred and the scorn were real enough though, even if diluted in certain minds. Anyway, at the time, the Pistols' notorious manager did nothing to alter the sentiment. His band hated Pink Floyd and that was all there was to it. Therefore all punks hated Pink Floyd.

Yet it was not only the odour of decaying musical forms that made young noses twitch in the middle of the seventies. Progressive rock was lambasted in its time due to something dear to many British hearts, the issue of class. Many groups such as Genesis, featuring four virtuoso musicians and a virtuoso front man who wore masks and costumes on stage, came from privileged backgrounds. Genesis formed at Charterhouse school, an educational establishment for posh boys (and, from 1971, a few girls). It was not quite the same for Pink Floyd, but working-class viewers only had to listen to Roger Waters arguing with Hans Keller on national television to grasp that Waters was not one of them. He had an accent and he sounded educated, for all that he was standing up to an even more elevated manifestation of class snobbery. Yes, meanwhile, emerged from the trippy, dippy heart of psychedelia.

In the seventies, Britain was still only a few steps away from the hidebound, permanent, stratified system of social ranking called class that had been instituted after the end of the feudal system, and which by the Industrial Revolution was British society's most notable feature. In a nutshell, there was the working class, the middle class, and the upper class. A classic comedy sketch with Ronnie Corbett (small), Ronnie Barker (medium) and John Cleese (tall) made it all crystal clear. Ronnie Corbett, the guy in the cloth cap and scarf… he knew his place. That place was at the bottom of the pile. In those days meritocracy was unknown, for there was virtually no movement between the classes. All was preordained. A youth born into the working class of any British town or city was as good as guaranteed to die in that class, albeit that ascent into the middle class became a possibility as the central portion of the British population expanded.

Progressive rock, therefore, was seen as middle class or even upper class. Certainly Genesis were perceived as upper class, because Charterhouse was a boarding school. A vast mass of plebians on the other hand went to ordinary schools in Britain, down the road maybe, or a bus ride away, perhaps reached on a grotty old pushbike. They were not transported in cars and their school place was free. They were working or middle class. Yet even progressive rock's middle-class heroes were somehow a cut above the lads and lasses of a standard British town. Prog stank of privilege, even if that privilege was mild, and earned. The working class laboured, struggled with poverty, lived in tower blocks, were on the dole. Working class dads were coal miners, steelyard workers or dockers. Little of that applied to much of the middle class. That, at least, was the perception; and thus another root of punk's rage bored itself into the fertile soil of class-ridden British society.

Moreover, the typical prog song – say, *And You And I* by Yes off their career high point *Close To The Edge* – was at least half a side of vinyl, consisted of movements strung together into a whole, utilised a battery of novel synthesizers, in the case of Yes played by a man in a cape, and, if the listener was lucky, could be followed lyrically. Not that Jon Anderson's lyrics did make sense very often. This progressive songwriting style was anathema to punks. Four minutes was too long for a song. Keyboards of any description were out. Solos were banned, unless they were just a few bars and consisted of one or two notes. Punks had no use for a thesaurus when they wrote lyrics; their songs were about their experiences of living, all of them vivid in their memories. They had neither beards nor moustaches with which to fiddle whilst pondering, as Jon Anderson did, a lengthy footnote at the bottom of a page of *The Autobiography Of A Yogi* by Paramahansa Yogananda. Ironically, progressive rock musicians wished to avoid predictable choruses and song structures in their music, which was a move away from light, standard pop. But punks were having none of that. Three minutes and the truth was all they needed.

Not all prog groups were as high minded as Yes, and as with punk the progressive scene had variety within it. Even Pink Floyd, the bitter enemy, sang about real world problems: capitalism and the capitalist mindset on *Animals,* isolation and regret on *Wish You Were Here,* madness, passing time and English society on *The Dark Side Of The Moon.* Though these concerns were set into music of beauty and symphonic complexity, they were at least the concerns of a proportion of the British people, rendered into elegant stanzas by Roger Waters. The number of Brits who had read *The Autobiography Of A Yogi* by Paramahansa Yogananda was much smaller. King Crimson meanwhile sat on the fence, with some songs about Moon

Children and princes called Rupert, elsewhere songs about society and strippers. But anyway, punk was not so much about thinking. It was about *feeling*. The energy of punk rock came from emotion, not concepts of liberal, humanist politics. Songs therefore were the emotional truth: the howl of rage, the constant dull ache of repressed anger, the occasional outburst of fury on rubbish-filled streets.

That being the case, in punk rock there was far less emphasis on melody than in other genres, including pop offshoots of the time like glam rock. Jon Anderson and Chris Squire were the melodic heart of Yes, able to write gorgeous tunes; ditto for Steve Hackett and Tony Banks of Genesis. David Gilmour and Richard Wright meanwhile were also fine melodists. Punk being sourced in an entirely different milieu, the vocals of Dave Vanian of The Damned for instance were more like a cross between speaking and singing, with pitch changes echoing chord changes, although he could hold a tune when the band had one. Melody had a small place in punk rock. Intonation of singing – the ups and down of a human voice when speaking about something important to them – were echoed in the snarled vocals of the typical punk song. Johnny Rotten followed this format, as did many other front men. For some punks though, tunes were considered too close to rejected musical genres, therefore to be dismissed.

Instrumentation was also key. Punk being in essence a working-class, anti-establishment movement, very few individuals had money for the latest Moog, a Solina string synthesizer or that bastion of prog, a mellotron. They had a scuzzy drumkit, a couple of microphones, electric bass and guitar, and the amps to go with them. That was all they could afford. In 1976 there was simply far less stuff in the world than there is now, and far less disposable income with which to buy it, a fact as true for musical instruments as for kitchen white goods. Therefore, punk bands – most often a quartet – took the standard pop rock format of drummer, bassist, guitarist and vocalist. They rejected anything else as too redolent of genres they wanted to ignore, prog most of all. No true punk band could have a keyboard player, which was one reason why, when the Stranglers began getting attention in punk circles and released their jaw-dropping 1977 debut *Stranglers IV: Rattus Norvegicus*, they were told they were not punks, they were freeloaders. Dave

Greenfield and his synthesizers belonged elsewhere. Punk was a bandwagon that group had no permission to jump onto.

Nor did punk bands have access to engineers or recording studios like Abbey Road. Theirs was a twilight world of cellar studios, tiny cubicles, beer-stained gear and tangled microphone cables. A studio available on their budget might have a sixteen-track reel to reel machine and mixing desk, but, then again, what punk band actually required all of those sixteen tracks? There was nothing to fill them up with. As for automatic double tracking, that was a meaningless concept to vocals drawled, snarled or growled.

For punks, their instruments were a means to an end. For prog rock musicians, their instruments were also objects upon which virtuosic skills could be displayed; the end itself. That even applied to drum kits. The abyss in the understanding of the place of instruments and studios in music separated the old from the new, the drum solo from the clash of cymbals. Steve Jones' attitude to his electric guitar was a world away from Steve Howe's. Howe could play upwards of four dozen notes per second. Jones played abrasively. Some punk guitarists at the beginning of their careers could not play even the basic barre E chord shape, tuning their guitar strings so that one finger laid across the fretboard played a major chord, and all they had to do then was remember where that finger went. But that was one of the points of punk. *Anyone* should be able to do it – be in a band, take up an instrument, shout out the truth. Virtuoso skill was anti-punk. It reeked of exclusivity and privilege.

Progressive rock, however, was not the only music genre rejected by punks. The glam rock of the early seventies was also suspicious, with its call to a specific teenage female audience, its scent of hippies typified by the Sweet, and its overall lack of realism and heart. True, David Bowie was a man apart; but he was not a band, though he did go around with one. Gary Glitter and his band seemed to come from some mutated, aluminium foil encrusted Edwardian pier show; music as music hall entertainment. That was not punk. Of course, many of the glam bands were from lower class backgrounds, as typified by Slade. But unlike Slade, who adored the limelight, some punk bands would never go on *Top Of The Pops,* at the time the only music outlet on national television, because that would be selling out. For politically aware bands such as The Clash, not going on *TOTP* was an article of faith. Neither did the Sex Pistols make that momentous move into the weird, pastel-hued, twee world of seventies British television.

Many musicians realised events were changing so quickly they were in danger of being left behind. Neil Young in his classic 1978 song *Hey Hey, My My (Into The Black)* referenced Johnny Rotten and the transformation punk was bringing to traditional rock music: *The king is gone but he's not forgotten, This is the story of Johnny Rotten. It's better to burn out than it is to rust…* Young's lyrics referred to the king (Elvis Presley, who had died the previous year) and Johnny Rotten, the former as a rocker whose legacy would live on, the latter as somebody whose sudden appearance on the scene could make Young, and by implication others, irrelevant. Even then, in 1978, Young was concerned about being left behind by unexpected changes in music, as evinced by the increasingly un-Young-like albums he recorded during the 1980s. He felt Johnny Rotten was a symbol of a kind of cultural erosion – the rust of the lyric – that might turn him into a staid, static figure of the past. And he did not want that fate. Yet the appearance of the Sex Pistols challenged him, and he felt he needed to find a response if he was to remain interesting and relevant.

Other musicians felt the same call. It was no accident that in 1978 Yes released *Tormato,* an album of comparatively short songs housed in a dreadful cover not designed by Roger Dean, Genesis released *And Then There Were Three,* also cutting down on song length, and Rush, having released the somewhat stodgy *Hemispheres* in 1978, upped their game to create a slew of superlative song-based albums starting with *Permanent Waves.* The writing had been on the wall for these groups after 1977. Some responded to that punkish graffiti, others did not. But there was no doubting that the times were changing.

One final aspect of punk music turned out to be significant. Until 1976 there were almost no female bands, just female artists, exploited, presented and ripped off by the overwhelmingly male music business. Female bands were an aberration because it was all about the boys bonding in their bands and the girls being the audience. Much pop music from the dawn of the genre had been arranged to cater for teenage girls, so it was unsurprising that this trend continued, but when punk exploded onto the scene there were more women musicians willing to give the democratising movement a try.

They, after all, also lived on litter-strewn streets and in tower blocks. They also had thoughts, feelings and voices. They had something to say. With new, cheap recording studios available and, as the years went by, a general trend towards more disposable income, being in a band of like-minded women became a viable option, as opposed to staying alone, selling appearance and sexuality, and being abused and manipulated by unscrupulous men. So it was that in Britain bands such as The Slits emerged, and in America, The Runaways.

The music of the decade before punk was what the movement rejected. It discarded the entirety of prog and much of what else lay around. It was a Year Zero movement in music, an anti-establishment rant set to imperfectly tuned guitars and smashed-up drums. It sidetracked the music business as far as it could, but that gave the more successful bands a problem. To get a single out, still more a vinyl LP, they had to negotiate with a potential enemy – record labels. In the 1970s, there were not too many of them, and most of the ones available were vast corporations. Yet part of the punk ethos was D.I.Y., and with an increase in equipment, a new emphasis on media, especially radio and television, and plenty to rail against, more chances to be heard were appearing.

And there were chinks in that corporate armour, even at the BBC. On Radio 1, the soft tones of John Peel began mentioning punk and all things associated. Radio 1 was huge and national – a critical asset to any punk band. John Peel's sessions, legendary even at the time, now became an essential line on the typical punk band's to-do list. There were also some record labels willing to give the new bands a chance, even though their ultimate motive was to piggyback the movement in order to make money from high record sales driven by novelty and media exposure. EMI was one of those record labels. But for some bands, that was okay. They needed to be heard. Their messages were important, their anger real, their intentions sincere. There was also a tier of labels with different corporate histories, such as Virgin Records. One problem with that label was the prog connection. Still, it was a chance; one grab for success. Time was passing and the moment was now.

In the words of Johnny Rotten: *we mean it, maaaaan.*

Chapter 3

Broken Britain

And what was it exactly in British society that the punk movement objected to? It was tradition, the status quo, the establishment, royalty, deference, the class system - conservatism in Britain went in many guises.

There were two major political parties, opposing one another like sclerotic, bovine wrestlers across the despatch box, with the Liberal Party an almost invisible addition, alongside a few other rag-taggle individuals. Though Labour was the natural party of the working class, they were far from ideal representation, and not in power as often as "the natural party of government," the Conservatives. But that party had only just taken one step away from Eton, Harrow and the like in the pompous form of Edward Heath. It was utterly hidebound, sure of its place at the top of the British tree, and never short of a penny or two. Moreover, it benefitted most from the antiquated first past the post electoral system. Labour, by contrast, though they had firebrand politicians and plenty of righteous zeal, struggled in a nation blinkered by such social traditions.

The media was similarly split. Most newspapers were right leaning, with the *Guardian* and the *Daily Mirror* to the left. Radio and television too, with the exception of ITV media controlled by the behemoth BBC, were bastions of tradition, where it was deemed daring for entertainers like Mike Yarwood to impersonate Harold Wilson. Occasionally they would commission a drama like Robert Lindsay's *Citizen Smith*, or a gritty social drama, but these were very much the exception, and in the case of the former were intended to laugh at rebels and revolutionaries as much as to portray British life. Book publishing was by and large a men's club based in London, with magazines elsewhere devoted to housewives and fast cars. There was an underground, and there was a counterculture, but at the somewhat chaotic free festivals of the early seventies that movement was more interested in getting laid and stoned whilst watching Hawkwind. The more politically active members of the underground were regularly harassed for their views and lifestyle. Rejecting tradition in seventies Britain was fraught with difficulties.

Britain, moreover, was racist, sexist and prejudiced. Many of its institutions turned a blind eye to these horrors. Where it mattered – the judiciary, the police, politicians and the military – British society was male dominated, white and entitled. For those male, white youths growing up in tower blocks (and a tiny number of non-white individuals too) who objected to that assumption of natural governance and automatic rights, there was something worth raging at. But the police did not care about punks and their worldview, except in that it afforded them plenty of opportunity for making arrests; nor did anybody else care, at first, except the esteemed members of the music press. The "silent majority" did not want their peace disturbed by youths with dayglo spiky hair and safety pins. That look was problematic. But suddenly punks were everywhere, including on the front page of their newspapers and in news reports; and it was all danger, danger, danger.

1973 was not a great year for Britain. Prime Minister Edward Heath spearheaded the nation joining the European Economic Community, which came into effect on the first day of the year; and that seemed a step forward to some. But strikes in February, IRA bombs in London, and VAT arriving on April Fools' Day were not so positive, and there were more strikes in May over pay restraints, while September saw an expansion of the IRA bombing campaign. In October, Ted Heath announced further pay restraints, while December saw the institution of the Three-Day Week, a measure reacting to industrial action brought by coal miners and railway workers. The first oil crisis, meanwhile, resulted in huge increases in the price of petrol.

With Tories in power, the unions felt they had an opponent to bring to account. Conserving electricity supplies during the Three-Day Week involved many public sacrifices, including using candles when the lights went out. The shock at seeing petrol prices skyrocket was palpable. No young person living in Britain in 1973 forgot the consequences of this economic and political chaos. There was an air of flailing instability in the air, which even the jolly antics of Slade and Wizzard on *Top Of The Pops* did little to distract from, at least, for those old enough to have jobs and mortgages. Industrial relations in particular were a running sore – a nasty, grim battle between the unions, representing the working class, and the Tories, representing big business.

Nor was 1974 much better. January was a recession month and there were more IRA bombs, while in February, trying to draw a line under the coal miners' dispute, Ted Heath called a general election. A hung parliament ensued – causing a stalemate and aggravation. After failing to make a pact with the Liberal Party, Heath resigned and Harold Wilson stepped in to form a minority Labour government. In March, the Three-Day Week and the miners' strike concluded. But there was a state of emergency now in Northern Ireland, the National Front gained support in parts of London, and there were appalling bombings in Dublin and Monaghan. June brought street clashes in London, while October brought another general election. Yet this national poll was far from decisive, Wilson only slightly improving his position. Inflation, meanwhile, rose to high levels and there were further bomb outrages, leading to the Prevention Of Terrorism Act.

1975 felt to many like more of the same, although one event of the time would have major repercussions – the arrival of Margaret Thatcher as leader of the Tories. There were National Front rallies, more bombs, the Moorgate Tube disaster, unemployment breaking the one million barrier, pay rises being limited, inflation peaking at 24.2%, the third Cod War, and Ross McWhirter shot dead by the IRA.

On 6 November, a band called Sex Pistols made its first public appearance under that name.

1976 was no less momentous, with further extremist outrages, the resignation of Harold Wilson, Direct Rule in Northern Ireland, local council election disappointment for Labour, the Yorkshire Ripper murders, and further industrial strife.

To many observers, Britain looked like a ragged, limping, messed-up nation. It was fragmented, with some parts at war with themselves, notably in London where the National Front were trying to stir up as much trouble as they could. Recollections now are of curtailed television broadcasting, cold weather or devastating droughts, filthy streets, strikes, riots, darkness, bleakness and gloom. Every corner seemed filled with windblown litter, every gutter with nameless gunk. While those memories may now be coloured by the mid-seventies air of malaise, they were true enough for any less fortunate individual or family eking out the wage, dole or pension of the time. This was a decade of discontent. It was blackout and turmoil without the balancing wartime feelings of national defence and endurance. It was just *grim:* endlessly, tediously grim. People at the bottom of the pile felt hopeless, and that made them angry. The psychological barrier of one million unemployed brought a particular brand of gloom, with men – still deemed the workers of the family unit – either fomenting trouble as best they could or too depressed to bother.

This too was an era of class war. The distinctiveness of each of the three classes was still obvious at the time, in part because affluence had yet to make the middle class as bloated as it was destined to become, but also because, not least in media eyes, the upper class was to be deferred to and the working class was to be suppressed. Working class living conditions in particular generated individual and community anger. In part, this was based on exploitation, injustice and inequality. But with the unions' organisation the TUC, who at the time wielded enormous power, agreeing to the Social Contract in an attempt to contain the economic crisis facing the nation, there were twisting loyalties, impossible dilemmas, and any number of shut doors facing the typical *Daily Mirror* reader. It really *was* war – the plebs versus the posh. This war took place on streets, in print and at work. It was *I'm Alright, Jack* with a knuckleduster.

One particular situation epitomised this mixture of volatile emotions and seething discontent. At the Grunwick photograph processing centre in North London, the anti-union stance of the right wing owner led to a number of unionised Asian women being sacked. This resulted in a series of violent confrontations between the police and thousands of employees outside the centre itself, battles which, stoked up by right-wing media day after day, brought a sense of impending civil war – a true class war. Gossip about private anti-union groups poured more fuel upon these fires.

By the autumn of 1976, the British economy seemed to teeter on the edge of an abyss. Even the elected representatives of the left, the Labour Party itself, was beginning to wonder if this new notion called monetarism might be the answer to the national dark ages they faced. Public spending should be restrained. Jim Callaghan, meanwhile, told his party conference that they could no longer spend their way out of a recession – a shocking statement to those who heard it. In the end, the International Monetary Fund granted Britain billions of pounds against a similar, lesser cut in domestic spending. But still the atmosphere of financial and social crisis weighed heavy upon the nation.

That atmosphere started seeping into the minds of the nation's youth as autumn arrived. The Sex Pistols had been around for a few months, as had The Damned. On 22 October that band released their debut *New Rose* – a punk rock single in name and truth. On 26 November the Sex Pistols' debut *Anarchy In The U.K.* was released. This was the explosion. This was the noise and the fury. It would be a wild ride from now on.

Yet the establishment that punk rock railed against was not only political. That establishment's upper class featured a juicy target resting in ermine-swathed comfort at the very top of the tree: the royal family. In the seventies, that collection of individuals could not be maligned in public, unless you were of a particular academic or political creed – a Communist, say. Queen Elizabeth II and her various descendants were unassailable, protected by the usual British unwritten rules. They were a family apart – a different species, almost. It was unthinkable to the overwhelming majority of the British public that a movement of scumbag nonentities wearing ripped clothes and wielding electric guitars should arrive, then speak the truth about royal power. What right did they have? This was the *Queen.* She was the epitome of Great Britain.

Yet punks did speak truth to royalty. In a class system as hidebound as that of Britain all unearned status was something to attack. That automatic privilege, acquired by nothing more strenuous than being born into the right family, was a feature of injustice – a tenet of the class war. The working class worked. The upper class lounged. Royalty lounged in furs.

Conveniently for royalty, it did not have to reply – another unwritten British rule. Had Prince Charles asked a punk in late November 1976, "And what do you do?" the answer might have been a snarled, "Blow up your palace." Punks were angry, and they cared nothing about who knew that. In fact, most punks – the Sex Pistols, for instance, managed by the unctuous Malcolm McLaren – *wanted* the media to know about their movement, their anger, their philosophy. Shouting at silence was a lonely affair. So punks were going to exploit every opportunity to make as much phlegm-soaked noise as possible. Shock tactics. If nobody was allowed to say anything anti-royal in public, punks were going to say exactly that; and their truth would hurt all the more for being unsayable.

But getting punk rock heard beyond pubs and clubs was problematic to its early, movement-defining bands, since that meant negotiating with the enemy. EMI, for instance, was a colossal organisation, a global corporation, which in 1976 already had forty-five years of success behind it. Yet for the fans of the Sex Pistols, now regularly gigging and getting music press attention, EMI was a fortress of the enemy. It reeked of privilege, capitalism, and huge amounts of money. But to release a single, even an LP, a punk band would have to sit down and negotiate with men coming from social circles way out of their experience. That was where having a good manager helped. The Sex Pistols had Malcolm McLaren and The Damned had Andrew Czezowski, a figure of crucial importance to the nascent punk scene. Czezowski was heavily involved in the London scene, especially through the Roxy Club, which in late 1976 began to feature many of the early punk bands. But that was comparatively early in punk's arc, and although the word was in regular use it did not yet quite apply to the movement. Nonetheless, Czezowski and The Damned could see that something was about to explode.

As it happened, Czezowski departed The Damned after a punk festival in France, leaving the band to usher in various new managers through their revolving door. But by now, journalists outside of *Sounds,* the *NME* and *Melody Maker* – all supportive of the punk scene and its standout bands – were beginning to pick up on the shock value of the scene. The British establishment was about to discover that a ragged, skint, angry mob of young people were anti them. That great British monolith, which had been in existence for centuries, was about to face an outburst of vitriol.

Chapter 4
New Rose

It is debatable that The Damned's first single *New Rose* was "punk's first single," as is generally thought, since earlier American bands had songs out that could perhaps fit that category. But *New Rose* was without doubt the first single marketed as punk rock in Britain.

The Damned of that debut 45 were a motley quartet composed of Dave Vanian, real name David Lett, Brian James, a.k.a. Brian Robertson, Captain Sensible, real name Raymond Burns, and Rat Scabies, also known as Chris Millar. Vanian was the singer and front man, whose rich baritone voice graced the two minutes and forty seconds of *New Rose.* Sensible was the bassist, though later he would move on to guitar duties. Brian James was the guitarist and Scabies sat behind the drum kit. The band formed in 1976 from Masters Of The Backside, in which Vanian, Scabies and Sensible had their early experiences in music. Chrissie Hynde was also a member of that band. Brian James meanwhile was the guitarist of London SS, a band with a checkered history which gifted the punk movement several of its stellar characters. Scabies and James were acquaintances, and soon enough they decided their best move was to form their own band. Scouting for a vocalist, only Vanian showed up to audition. Sensible was the fourth part of the jigsaw. In due course the quartet decided to name themselves The Damned.

These were lads from the underside of London. Scabies could be found sweeping floors to get money, while Sensible was a bog brush jockey at the Fairfield Halls. Chris Millar received his stage name after getting scabies from a rat. Meanwhile, Vanian's day job was obvious once his black make-up came into view. He was a gravedigger. Indeed, it was commonly observed that he smelled of the grave. So, as with all bands in that chaotic year for music in the capital city, there were brief alliances before the coalescing of The Damned, arguments and disappointments amid a roster of bands with no hope and other bands with lots.

Gigging in London through 1976, The Damned soon attracted a coterie of fans, all energised by the nascent punk movement. Their debut gig occurred in July, supporting the Sex Pistols at the 100 Club in Oxford Street. Soon they were looking for a record deal of some sort. They were young, and all they wanted was to ride the punk wave while it lasted. They had no pretentions and no expectation that the ride would last long. They were out to enjoy themselves. That said, not all audiences were enamoured of Captain Sensible and his antics. According to James in an interview given to *The Guardian* in 2018, the band were disliked, chased by motor bike gangs, assembling on stage some nights to deliver little more than musical chaos.

They were no ordinary punks, however. Although the movement's current enemy was the recent musical past – glam and prog, primarily – the B side of *New Rose* was a cover of The Beatles' *Help.* Moreover, this quartet were decent musicians, not least Vanian, one of rock's great front men, and James, whose guitar work, though chainsaw rough, was of a high calibre. Scabies meanwhile had a drumming technique that was ninety percent cymbals and ten percent the other parts of the kit – more an assault than a playing technique. As for Sensible, he turned out to be a lover of that musical past, a fan of John McLaughlin, who mockingly referred to himself as "a hippie with teeth." Yet combined, and fuelled by the new movement, this was a band with a huge amount to offer its fans, not least wild, wild energy.

It was Dave Robinson and Jake Riviera of Stiff Records (also appearing for the first time in 1976) who offered The Damned the record deal they wanted. This label's roster included a who's who of punk, and, a couple of years later, New Wave. *New Rose* was released on 22 October of that year, five weeks before a musical incendiary of equivalent significance: *Anarchy In The U.K.*

The song was a classic written by James. A guitarist of imagination and style, he had accumulated a number of riffs and chord sequences during his time in London SS and his other band, Bastard. When he and Scabies got together to work on the track, it was Scabies' drumming that made everything gel. James' ex-bandmates had complained about Scabies' dishevelled appearance and wonky hair, but James saw through all that. The combination of Scabies and himself was *powerful.*

So it was that Stiff Records signed The Damned for their debut single. Recorded in a single day at London's tiny eight-track Pathway Studios, it was produced by Nick Lowe, himself on the roster of Stiff Records and a highly regarded musician with a few hit singles of his own. Somehow, despite the implausibility of the band members' characters, and despite the chaos of the scene, Lowe managed in these difficult circumstances to capture the energy of the band when they played together. James later recalled that they spent more time in the pub around the corner, while Lowe, a studio veteran, worked on the technical stuff.

The B-side cover of *Help* sounded like it had taken an overdose of speed. It lasted one minute and thirty-seven seconds – a minute less than the A-side. Delivered with snarling panache, it was no homage to the past, though secretly Sensible at least recalled that sunshine era with pleasure. James at the time considered his new band to be a sped-up rock 'n' roll outfit. Yet it was more, as he would find out. It was the A-side where the action really was.

"Is she really going out with him?"

Vanian, messing around in the studio in front of a live mike, uttered that immortal line from Motown's 1964 Shangri-Las classic, a song he loved. But this was twelve years later, London, and the world was very different. Yet that line in retrospect acts as a pivot around which the music of punk moved, mocking the past, rejecting it, for all that Vanian himself wished for no such thing. Before *New Rose* there was Motown and psychedelia. Then: *Is she really going out with him?* Then, punk rock.

The opening riff is a classic on a level with those of the Sex Pistols, delivered with spiky overdrive and a fresh glow. The drums sound like battle drums, preparing for war. Then it all peaks and there is a grunted "Ungh!" from Vanian, before the second riff begins, leading into the song proper. Vanian sings as if he is out of breath, a bravura performance of rushed intensity. For the film made at the time (3,500,000 views on YouTube) his face is right up against the camera, and already he is using some of his visual performance quirks, such as looking from left to right between lines as he takes a breath. Scabies meanwhile drums half naked and smoking a fag, while Sensible wears the white plastic sunglasses which would in later times characterise him. The film is utterly compelling: organised chaos, manic and intense. At the end of the song everything dissolves into a strident ocean of cymbals, at once bringing the chaos of raw sound and defining one of Scabies' techniques.

The lyrics were not exactly a love song (the band would later deliver a stone-cold classic with exactly that title), though they did reference the thrill of new partnerships. James, who wrote the lyrics as well as the music, was referring to the excitement that he felt about the new movement when he wrote: *I got a feeling inside of me, it's kinda strange like a stormy sea.* He could hardly believe he was part of so strong a scene. Everyone around punk could see it was no dalliance with gimmickry. This was the real thing.

Vanian, meanwhile, was in theory second shot at prospective vocalist for The Damned after Sid Vicious, but Vicious never turned up to audition. As it happened, James had spotted Vanian in the audience of various of his gigs, and considered this vision of goth a front man. "You look like a singer," he told Vanian. As Vanian recalled in the 2018 *Guardian* interview, punk was more of an individualist's ethic before the explosion of spiky hair and ripped clothes which characterised its public fashion statement. He turned up for the audition in winklepickers, basing his black-clad look on horror films. But his vocal for the song could not be bettered, those distinctive tones apparent from the start.

The band were poverty-stricken, living from week to week, bombing up and down Britain's motorways to play gigs and record more tracks. Vanian was no longer a gravedigger and Scabies did not have time to sweep floors. As for the porcelain at Croydon's Fairfield Halls, that got new cleaners. The Damned, fuelled by speed and cider, were here for the ride.

Andrew Czezowski managed The Damned up to the day after the First International Punk Festival at Mont De Marsan in France, which took place half way through August 1976. I asked him about those times.

I had no experience and did no planning – I personally like that, thinking on my feet. Any act starting out doesn't have much experience either, so having an inexperienced manager is par for the course. With luck, both the manager and the band grow as needed. The only plan I had at the time was to get gigs and reviews. Once a solid base of gig and reviews was under our belt, I would have had contact with record companies, which is the short term goal… ££££££.

I wondered if Czezowski felt he had good luck with The Damned.

I don't think it's so much luck, as connections – being in the know. I think all start-ups and new bands are alike, that they gravitate towards one another because they are all chasing the same dream as outsiders. But I had separated with the band on our return trip from Mont De Marsan, 22nd August 1976.

For all the brilliance of Dave Vanian as a front man, James as a guitarist and songwriter, and the Captain too, it seemed that a lot of The Damned's sheer energy and power came from Scabies' unique drumming style. I wondered whether Czezowski felt the same.

Yes, he was powerful, similar to Keith Moon. He attacked those drums, had complete control: no fear! 'New Rose' is a good example.

Was the recording venue for that single a bit of a dive?

Actually it was quite pleasant, it was a clean coal hole painted white, but a little damp, and only room for one person plus band.

Czezowski in his book about the Roxy Club described himself as not disappointed by record company rejections.

I always thought they were wrong and that it would only be a question of time. I felt that as more gigs and more ground swell came, the record companies would come to me. But that never happened, as the band and I parted company in August. Record companies are full of sheep, following what others do and trying to jump on the bandwagon. I think we saw that – a common story.

Czezowski was regarded as a mellow and level-headed man. Brian James thought well of him. I wondered whether he ever got tired of the band members' high jinks.

> *Not until Mont De Marsan. My style and goal was to manage a great rock band, I didn't think I should be one of them; my role was to coordinate, deal and sell their talent. I didn't feel I should be hanging around in studios overseeing – they do the music, I do the management. Jake Riviera was the opposite: booze/coke/speed, etc – standard rock'n'roll management style, and not for me. If the band hadn't dumped me first it could easily have gone the other way, mainly driven by Rat.*

The response to punk's first single was enthusiastic. Already, many of the journalists at the nation's music rags were inserting themselves into the scene, befriending bands, writing live reviews and articles, promoting this, supporting that. *Sounds, NME* and *Melody Maker* were all into punk from the beginning, and played a huge part in its sudden stamping on the nation's toes. It was apparent to many that, although punk bands often had some of their roots in Britain's beer-stained R&B music and its American equivalent, punk, as epitomised by *New Rose,* was something entirely new. It was visceral and vibrant. In fact, it took a chainsaw to R&B. Of course, a few critics turned their noses up at that, since it seemed to them that the denim-clad charisma of the British R&B scene – mostly based in the pub circuit – was being hacked about into something more basic. But that was one of the points of punk rock. It *was* a return to basics. Moreover, it *enjoyed* slashing those R&B roots, burning that heritage in a three-minute blast of toxic riffola.

This, after all, was music for young people, and that meant music for those wanting to find out who they were – the search for identity. Regardless of the lyrics, regardless of what television news programmes were beginning to show of punk rock, the music was unmistakable in its raucous power. It was distilled energy, and if there was one thing British youth had in abundance with which to rail against the establishment of their times, it was energy. The debut single by one of the movement's star bands spoke of rushing forward, of rebelling, of being somebody brand new in the adult world. It was a call to arms.

The adult world is confusing to adults as well as to adolescents. The Damned were as yet too youthful to realise that, but what they did sense were the possibilities of the chance life had offered them. They had the guitars, the drums and a compelling vocalist. They had a fantastic debut 45, and already the reception was positive.

New Rose did not trouble the British pop charts, though its equally manic follow up *Neat Neat Neat* climbed to number 52. The band were also first to release a punk album, their mesmerising debut *Damned Damned Damned,* released by Stiff Records on 18 February 1977, which managed to reach number 34 – quite an achievement, but also indicative of the speed with which punk was beginning to make waves.

That debut single was on the debut album, and Chris Welch of the *NME* thought highly of the LP. Remarking on the musical talents of the quartet (an irony not lost on subsequent generations), he reserved his most eloquent praise for Brian James, calling him "the most effective powerhouse guitarist since Pete Townshend." The album as a whole he considered notable and convincing; a leader in its field. Yet when *Damned Damned Damned* was released, James was just 22 years old. He had been caught up in a whirlwind, and the band were reaping the benefits. Their collective ethos was to enjoy those benefits to the maximum extent on the assumption that they would not last long.

West Country acid-guitarist Icarus Peel recalled meeting these four young men.

> *As I remember, it was a sunny, hazy weekend many lifetimes ago when we slipped down to Hastings from South London for a break. We were gently tripping in a pub late on, smoke, noise and a loud jukebox; perhaps it was a lock-in. The four sitting at the table were instantly recognizable: one ghoul, one punky leather jacket, one slightly deranged looking, and the Captain. We wandered over and became immersed in their corner of the Universe. Fairly quickly, the Captain wandered off with my friend, almost certainly in search of female company and adventure. I sat and listened to Rat talk fluently and apparently knowledgeably about various subjects from history to transport systems; a benign lecture almost. He was as animated as Dave was still. Mr Vanian sat practically silent, a little removed but not unfriendly, more vaguely amused at something in his own spectral psyche. Brian James and I had a long discussion on liberating guitars from music shops, a popular and respected hobby among us all. He was riddled with*

cockney; funny and sharp, a good guy. I vividly remember at one point floating above the table with Rat and wondering if he was on the same acid as me. The strange thing is, I am sure they bought all the drinks, although they were all bottles, so perhaps they had lifted a crate from behind the bar. I cannot remember saying good-bye. I woke to a salty symphony of sea on shingle beneath the pier. Neat…

In a June 1977 interview on Manchester's Piccadilly 261 Radio, Rat Scabies outlined the hinterland and state of the band around the release of *New Rose.* Punk, he said, was a label, and people have to put labels on everything (including radio), so he did not object to that. The music scene had become stagnant, and punk's energy changed what needed to be changed. Too many fat and rich bands had been hanging out in L.A. eating cheeseburgers. Quizzed about what *he* wanted, he admitted without hesitation that he wanted money and everything that went with stardom. But money changed bands. He himself was scruffy and dishevelled precisely because he had no money. His image came from necessity.

Punk, he continued, was huge. The Damned were the first punk band to hit America, and just before the interview he had returned from that country. Punk was big in America as well as in Britain. The kids there loved it.

Decadence, he continued, was what he and the others were aiming for – they made no bones about that. Their personal appearance was often due to poverty or simple bad luck. A lot of the attitude of punk, he explained, came from the dole queue. It was a case of trying to get rich quick, and he was pretty envious of the Sex Pistols getting onto the front cover of *NME.* That, in fact, was the inspiration for writing an early Damned classic *Stab Your Back.* There was jealousy, rivalry and enmity in punk, as well as working class solidarity.

New Rose, then, was not just an opening shot at the musical, cultural and political establishment. Though it followed the punk ethic, it was round one of a battle to get famous and filthy rich. The Damned had seen America, and it looked better than Britain. Maybe a new rose should bloom outside of Britain's shores.

The Damned's early gigs were exciting, sometimes chaotic, always memorable. I asked mega-fan Kevin Shepherd about those heady days.

My first ever Damned gig was back on 8 October 1976. It was the band's tenth gig – and they did have amp trouble! It was fifty pence to get in. I only had thirty-five pence, but Muddie the landlady let me in anyway. There were lots of older denim and leather-clad Status Quo and Steely Dan numbskulls in the crowd, and a few proto-punks and youngsters. Future members of UK Decay, the Exiles, who went on to be the Jets, and various football hooligans were present amongst the audience. The Damned played five numbers, then had amplifier problems, so there was a lull for about twenty minutes before then returned to play four of the five numbers again and two further tracks. At the time, we of course didn't know what the titles were.

Dave Vanian was very much the front man.

Vanian had blood capsules from the joke shop, spitting some at the audience. He also climbed on the tables that had been piled up to create a bigger space. He was like a whirling dervish, the Captain too, who at the time insisted on being called Johnny Sensible. After the gig, Captain decided to try and break into a local chemist shop – a large window was smashed. Incidentally, I did repay Muddie her extra fifteen pence some forty years later at a UK Decay reunion gig.

This was the beginning of a long love affair with the band.

A few more memories… I went with some older friends, who I played football with and went to watch Luton with. A couple of them had been at the Damned's Art College gig in July, after the Sex Pistols cancelled and Shanne my friend put the Damned on instead. A few of the older denim-clad punters threw beermats and peanuts at the Damned. The band were paid a flat fee of £40 for the gig, which was a lot more than they had previously got by all accounts. The older punters were shouting for Status Quo and Led Zep songs. Brian seemed older than the rest of the band, probably because he was – but they were all drinking at the bar before and after the gig, and chatted to anyone who wanted to talk. The second Damned gig I saw was at the Tiddenfoot Leisure Centre in Leighton Buzzard. The local Hells

Angels turned up to this one, and I thought it was a better gig, but again all the locals weren't so keen, being mainly boring old farts. Rat was on top form that night, but the local motorcycle gang – Madcaps as they were known – decided they wanted to fight everyone…

But not everyone was enamoured of this band's angry energy. For some, it was too much. Some simply could not relate. I spoke with Bill Sewell of Bill's Kitchen, who saw one of the earliest Damned gigs at the Marquee in London when he was fifteen.

I was going to school in Barnes at the time, and one of the local pubs, the Red Cow in Hammersmith, was a venue for the first punk bands. My mates used to go down there to see The Jam. I wasn't much of a fan of them myself. One day, my mate Paul told me he'd got tickets for The Damned at the Marquee, and did I want to go? I wasn't sure. I'd heard them on the radio and felt unsure about the music. I'm an optimistic person, and punk seemed pessimistic to me. I don't think I related to the anger in punk. I did like the Sex Pistols' 'God Save The Queen,' which I thought was witty, but I didn't want to listen to it. But I went anyway to the Marquee, and I hated it. I tried to pogo a bit, but it just didn't feel right. Anyway, at the end of the gig we were given a free Damned single. Outside on Wardour Street I smashed it in two across my knee and threw away the pieces. Punk was not for me. It didn't seem to have any beauty, any melody. It was just too angry for my taste.

Chapter 5

They Vibrate

The Vibrators were around before punk exploded. A quartet in traditional rock band mode, they comprised vocalist and songwriter Knox, drummer Eddie, with John Ellis on guitar and Pat Collier on bass. In 1976 they were already supporting (and backing on vinyl) the popular musician Chris Spedding, he of *Motor Bikin'* fame, at London's 100 Club. Spedding was a fixture on the British music scene, not only as an admired live performer but as a producer and session guitarist, where his sheer versatility on the instrument was apparent to all. It was Spedding who got the band signed, convincing RAK Records' Mickie Most to add them to his books. With indecent haste the band found themselves recording an early punk Peel session in autumn 1976, with a couple more recorded shortly after; and all this before the demise of the punk movement at the dawning of 1978.

It was not long before they were a headlining act, and at the 100 Club itself – a major venue of the time. Not only that, they played at the Roxy Club pioneered by Andrew Czezowski and his partner Susan Carrington, making punk history just weeks after the Pistols' Bill Grundy Show moment. One month later they would be supporting the iconic American artist Iggy Pop. Like The Damned, they were there when it all began.

The debut 45 was set to be *We Vibrate,* released around the same time as *Anarchy In The U.K.* and *New Rose.* It was written by bassist Collier, with a Knox-penned B-side *Whips And Furs,* a cut that would appear on the debut LP *Pure Mania.* That LP however would be released on Epic Records, with whom the band signed early in 1977.

The debut single was released in a stark red-and-white cover showing the band and the title in a slashed electric warning font. This design, like so many of the pioneering punk singles, was radically different from those which had preceded it. It spoke of haste, of simplicity, of directness. The music was both punky and redolent of the glam years, which by 1976 had begun to fade into rust and dulled tinsel. Opening with a bluesy guitar riff, it fell into a catchy verse and "C'mon everybody" chorus which itself harked back to previous years, and similar dance-along anthems. The chord work was reminiscent of Status Quo-style boogie, but overall the song *was* something different – rougher, spikier, with little by way of shine or complexity. It both announced the band and their manifesto, and paved the way for darker, grittier, music.

I spoke with Eddie (real name John Edwards) about the making of the single and his times with The Vibrators. First I asked him about the Roxy Club, where the band played three times during January and February 1977.

> *Boy, that was a long time ago. I just remember a small, low stage, and a small broom cupboard under the stairs to change in! There were always people like Joe Strummer there to check you out, and a very lively crowd. Downstairs, I think…*

I asked Eddie if he and the band felt like part of the punk scene, or whether, perhaps as with The Stranglers, they felt more like outsiders.

> *I felt like a member of the Vibrators. I felt we had our own thing, and were another different band to the others. We got on well with the other bands when we played with them, whoever it was. It always felt like the press were trying to put you into a box with a label. I wouldn't have thought The Stranglers felt outside it, but I may be wrong.*

Eddie then spoke about the making of the *We Vibrate* single. I asked if it was recorded in dire circumstances in some run-down studio, or somewhere more upmarket.

> *We recorded 'We Vibrate' with Mickie Most in Morgan Studios in London. That was a big studio, and he was a hugely successful producer at the time, with hits from the Jeff Beck Group, Suzi Quattro, The Animals and many other top groups from the '60s and '70s. Maybe a bit of glam rubbed off on it, but it wasn't put there deliberately. We did the session at the same*

time as we recorded 'Pogo Dancing' with Chris Spedding, as it was he who recommended us to Mickie Most.

The Vibrators soon signed to Epic Records, and I asked Eddie how that went. Did it feel good, or was the band uneasy about flirting with Big Business?

Most of the bands signed to big labels, as that was the only way to be successful in 1976–77. We wanted to be successful just like all the other bands at the time.

The Vibrators played at the legendary 100 Club Punk Special. I asked Eddie what it felt like playing there.

We felt at the time that it was a big show, but we didn't know we were to back Chris Spedding until he turned up to play. I think they advertised him to get people down without telling him. We were going through some songs in the office when The Damned were on, and Sid Vicious threw a glass which hit a pillar and went into a girl's eye, cutting it badly. Another guy was cut in the face. They were both brought to the office, and we looked after them until the ambulance arrived. When I went on, I looked down and my hands were covered in blood. I remember thinking: if this is what punk is all about, then count me out. We just wanted to be a rock 'n' roll band and have fun. The event was totally sold out, but most people left after us and Spedding, and I remember Buzzcocks playing to a small handful of people. But we knew that all the press were there and that we were at the start of something big.

The Vibrators recorded a very early John Peel punk session for that legendary disc jockey. I asked Eddie how it went, and whether the band met Peel himself.

That was great! The tracks were recorded at Maida Vale studios, and the producers and engineers were totally into any ideas we had, and got a great sound and performance out of us. I guess nearly everyone who worked there would say that. We didn't meet John Peel at the time, but did meet him some time later when we did a talk thing about punk for Radio 1. We were playing some songs from our second album, and he and Ray Davies were on a panel with Poly Styrene. The show was chaired by Jimmy Saville, who turned up, did his bit, then left without speaking to anyone. We had a long chat with John Peel and Ray Davies, who were both very complimentary and helpful. Let's face it, John Peel helped break more bands on the radio than all the other DJs put together!

Finally, I asked Eddie if he had any other strong memories of the time.

What I remember most is slogging round all the clubs in Britain and Europe. We had the feeling that this was our music and we were going to do it our way, and that the fans stuck by us and kept coming year after year even when there was no help from radio and press. Boy, it was just magic, and so much fun for me. I really felt we were pulling people together and making a difference. I still feel that.

Chapter 6

Anarchy

Rock music has seen its fair share of bad boys. That was a look for a few bands, whose audience consisted of teenaged girls and also other boys for whom they were potential role models. In the years preceding punk, this clear, financially beneficial model worked well for the bad boys and for the record companies who housed them. Yet almost all those bands were never *really* so bad. The Rolling Stones sang about shagging women and stuff, but that was within the bounds of most social norms, even the new, stretched, post-hippie ones. Led Zeppelin's secrets were still mostly secret, and they presented themselves as fantastic musicians first and foremost. On the nation's only pop music television show, *Top Of The Pops,* music was safe, usually twee, occasionally unusual. Radio 1, meanwhile, was the abode of DJs as much interested in themselves as in the music they were playing. That music took listeners to some strange places, but it was never dangerous. The whole bad boy, bad band look through the first half of the decade might have been denim clad or based on leathers, but it rarely deviated from the BBC norm, let alone Britain's deferential social norms. All was beige, bland and safe. Even Hawkwind were basically acid-loving chaps whose music chugged along. As for the free festival scene, that was very much underground, and was being watched by the police anyway. Big record labels and their media pluggers needed to balance their books, even when they took risks with musicians or groups who promised but might not deliver. Safety was important. There existed a social and cultural envelope around pop and rock music, whose extremities were not often tested.

All that changed in late 1975, when a band recently named Sex Pistols appeared in London and began gigging.

This band emerged from a trio of teenagers called The Strand, featuring Steve Jones as vocalist, though in the Sex Pistols he would play guitar. Paul Cook was the drummer, while guitar duties in this proto-Pistols line up were taken by Wally Nightingale. One of their hang outs was a clothes shop in London's King's Road, at the time called Too Fast To Live, Too Young To Die, an establishment run by Malcolm McLaren and Vivienne Westwood. By late 1974, Steve Jones had asked McLaren to become the band's manager, sensing an opportunity for progress and development. One new member joined the band at this point, the bass player Glen Matlock. An art student and fellow member of the King's Road shop crowd, Matlock also worked on occasion at the establishment, alongside Jordan, a young woman whose eclectic, striking style turned out to be punk before punk exploded.

McLaren and Westwood now decided to step away from their earlier Teddy Boy/Rocker look into something a bit more dangerous. The shop was renamed SEX, casting aside its retro threads and moving into the opposite corner of fashion, based in part on S&M gear. McLaren by now was becoming embroiled in the music scene of America as well as Britain, managing for a short period the influential band New York Dolls, an early member of the American punk scene alongside Iggy And The Stooges and others. Returning to the comparative calm of Britain, he decided Jones, Cook and Matlock, still calling themselves The Strand, might be worth developing into something akin to the New York Dolls.

Although the band had been practicing their chops and gigging, it transpired that Jones was not an easy fit into the role of front man, and felt ambivalent about his position there. With Nightingale departing, he took over guitar duties, leaving a large hole, into which some kind of charismatic, striking, punk-inspired front man would fit... but who?

McLaren knew roughly what he wanted. He tried to convince Sylvain Sylvain of the New York Dolls to step across the pond in order to front the band, but Sylvain, along with another possible, Richard Hell, declined. Various tales of urban legend describe the subsequent hunt for a new vocalist, including stopping likely individuals in London streets.

Then fate stepped in. In the summer of 1975, Bernard Rhodes, taking care of the musical direction of the band, spotted a gangly youth with green hair walking down the street. This youth (then only nineteen) was asked to audition for front man duties. Of particular note was his T shirt, which announced to the world that he hated Pink Floyd. Yet some kind of glamour surrounded this young man, and after the audition he was offered the job. To his enormous credit, he accepted. Already some of the band members were aware that John Lydon, as he was christened, was somehow *different.* As yet, however, they had little idea of how or why. According to Jones, John Lydon soon became Johnny Rotten, on account of his poor teeth. In that brief moment a sonic die was cast, setting up the conditions for a transformation in British music. The nation and its musical heritage would never be the same.

Accounts of when The Strand became Sex Pistols vary, but what is certain is that the band's first gig under that name occurred at St Martin's School Of Art, where Matlock was a student, in November 1975. They supported Bazooka Joe and played a variety of material, including some rock covers. Further gigs followed, and they began to acquire a following. The clothes changed. The songs kept coming. Some of them were extraordinary.

Anarchy In The U.K., with lyrics written by Lydon and music by the band, was premiered to the world live in Manchester on 20 July 1976. It was, of course, a lightning bolt from the Muses.

The tune is simple, but memorable; no one-note effort over changing chords. It is a curiosity of modern times that people describing a song or album almost exclusively refer to the lyrics, and indeed mix up the terms lyric-writing with songwriting, as though they were the same thing. The debut Sex Pistols single had a memorable *tune,* making it, even before the extraordinary lyrics and the band's image came into view, something a bit different. That was a critical part of its success. It was an earworm.

What propelled that earworm into something unforgettable even fifty years later was Lydon's vocal delivery. Given the chance events surrounding his arrival at the front of the band, so unique a vocalist could never have been improved upon. He was the only man for this recording.

At the time, because the Sex Pistols were so polarising, and because the establishment hated them, leading to endless media tussles, too little attention was given to Lydon's singing style. Yet with the benefit of hindsight it can be observed that he was quite exceptional. Although he snarled and growled and drawled the song's lyrics, the pitch modulation of his voice was intensely musical, as if he was engaging in vocalisations half way between speaking and singing. This style of delivery made it seem as though he *was* speaking – to working class kids. Yet when he reached the chorus, that style leaked out into something a little more melodic, bringing the anthemic conclusion of the song into sharper focus. Then there was his diction. Lydon has a particularly rich speaking voice, in part a product of his Irish background (though he was born in London, considers himself British, and spoke at school with an English accent). As the music of the Sex Pistols improved, and as Lydon developed his style and stage persona, this diction became exaggerated to remarkable effect, notably the way he rolled his rrrs. Every consonant was given due attention: the -st in *Antichrist,* the -ch- in *anarchiste.* Every nuance was devised, modulated and controlled into a bravura performance of unique intensity. It remains one of the outstanding vocals of rock music.

Lydon's stage persona was rooted in the trials of his own wretched upbringing and in his natural wit and intelligence. Upon meeting him, Steve Jones described him as "smart," belying the somewhat hunched appearance and bright green hair. But to hear the debut Pistols song was one thing. To see Lydon perform it was another. Raised in a poor, working-class area favoured by Irish and Jamaican communities, his was a life of pain at school owing to his natural shyness and anxiety. Spinal meningitis brought deep trauma to him at an early age, resulting in some of the characteristics of his appearance, notably the so-called "Lydon stare." These accidents of fate in an ordinary youth might have resulted in a life following the no-hope trajectory the punks were fighting against. In Lydon, they assembled to create a front man and vocalist likely never again to be seen. He *believed* in what he was writing about. He believed in his own feelings, much of which were inculcated into him by the remorseless, harsh conditions of his life, knee-deep in street rubbish and trampled down by the weight of the establishment he so despised. Punk and the Pistols was his chance to lash out against the system.

Lydon on stage was unforgettable. As Susan Carrington, one half of the team that created the Roxy Club, said in the book describing its life and times, all eyes were on Johnny Rotten when the Pistols were on stage. He was riveting.

> *John had this feral quality about him, and managed to express himself without being corralled – hence his very individual style.*

Virgin Records managing director Jon Webster also saw the Sex Pistols early in their career.

> *I saw them at Barbarella's in Birmingham on 14th August 1976. I sat there with my jaw on the floor, thinking, "What on earth is this?" This was not The Eagles. I was gobsmacked. I'd never seen anyone like Lydon challenging the audience from the stage, abusing them almost, in the way he did. They were a force – like a sledgehammer. It was something utterly different to anything that had gone before. I almost felt they weren't playing music, it was some "other" thing.*

I asked Simon Draper, former Head of A&R at Virgin Records, and the man who had Mike Oldfield, Tangerine Dream and numerous other groups signed to the trailblazing label, about his initial impressions of the Sex Pistols' music.

> *Their music at first I thought was just noise, indescribable really, but that was a knee jerk reaction. Malcolm McLaren was going around record companies playing their demo recordings, and I found him unpleasant and confrontational. I think my feelings about the music were as much about McLaren as anything. So I passed on them. I presume those were the Dave Goodman recordings. But I was at the time trying to change the Virgin Records style because I didn't want us to become typecast. I needed a rock 'n' roll act – like Slade, for instance. I wanted a change of image. That's why I signed The Motors, amongst other bands. When I heard the finished Chris Thomas recording of 'Anarchy In The U.K.' I immediately knew it was a hit.*

I asked Draper what he thought McLaren wanted.

> *I think he wanted a state of permanent anarchy. He wanted to subvert everything. What he really wanted to happen was for every record company to reject the Sex Pistols. McLaren rode roughshod over us at times, but he misjudged Richard Branson, perhaps because Richard stammered a bit, wasn't hip, and didn't know much about the music. But that was McLaren's mistake. Richard wanted the Sex Pistols for Virgin Records, and tried to*

get them after EMI dropped them. In the end, after A&M, they just fell into our lap.

There was another aspect to *Anarchy In The U.K.* which brought the band instant notoriety. So far, the bad boys of rock had actually been fairly safe, if imbued with a jocular misogyny and casual attitude to aggression. But it was pretty difficult to be afraid of them. The Sex Pistols on the other hand exuded such intense menace, had such a striking appearance, and cared so little about the moral panic they were starting, they *were* worth fearing. This was a truly frightening prospect, something to be terrified of from the perspective of the cosy middle class or the entitled establishment. Britain had never seen anything like this. Eyes raised upwards in worship of the royals and others of the superior professional classes, they had missed what was bubbling up throughout 1976. When it exploded half way through autumn of that year, they were unprepared for the onslaught. In Lydon's hypnotic, compelling, perfectly enunciated vocal they heard a call to arms from a community they had so far thought nothing of. It stank of class war. It was a cry of hate. Shock stunned them, and for a while they could not move. Anarchy was living again on the streets of London.

The lyrics of *Anarchy In The U.K.* were also of particular note. Lydon held nothing back when he wrote them. His aim was true: the fat bastards of finance, elitist politicians, and anybody else who called the establishment a home.

The opening lines set out his stall in language shocking at the time: *I am an Antichrist, and I am an anarchist.* He spat out those sibilant consonants, perverting the pronunciation of anarchist with brilliant precision: *anarchiste.* This was a paeon to destruction, a scream from the heart of suppressed, furious, working-class punks. He wanted to destroy, though he did not quite know how to do that. His aim seemed random, like some hideous gunman instigating a reign of terror. He felt like a dogsbody, so all he desired was anarchy – the full flight of chaos through the streets of Britain. Anarchy in Britain… right now.

In his line about the future dream being a shopping scheme, he mocked the soft, easy lives of infantile consumers, who at the time were a comparatively new invention. He saw that commercial teat with the same jaundiced, left-leaning eye as Erich Fromm and other humanist liberals, who not too many years earlier had pointed out the perils of unrestrained capitalism, particularly of the free market variety. This consumer obsession was akin to the unthinking suckling of babies. Post-war economics was infantilising human beings.

Lydon also set out the range of methods he would use to bring anarchy; to get exactly what he wanted. He asked how many ways to get what he wanted: *I use the best, I use the rest, I use the enemy, I use anarchy.* This was no holds barred declaration of intent, set against chainsaw guitars and a pounding beat, drawled in his inimitable, terrifying, sneering voice.

But there was more. Through the 1970s a campaign of bombings and shootings was waged by the I.R.A. and other terrorists, aiming for a range of targets, some of them symbolic of Britishness itself. Dozens of people died; a reign of horror for all those unlucky enough to be or to be near the victims. Northern Ireland was one setting for the campaign, but there were many British targets – even pubs. Yet Lydon referenced those intimate horrors in his lyrics: the M.P.L.A., the U.D.A., the I.R.A. He thought his country was the U.K. *Or just... another... country. Another council tenancy.* Lydon was himself of Irish extraction, his mother and father working-class immigrants from Ireland. So he knew where to place the blade. He knew where it would hurt.

The conclusion set the scene for chaos: *Get pissed, Destroy!* It was a nihilist agenda, a manifesto, the ultimate expression of independence and intent. In that regard, as in most others, it was phenomenal.

This trailblazing 45 was released in a plain black sleeve at the back end of 1976, when things looked bad for politics, the economy, industrial relations, and much else besides. It smashed aside the litter, the boredom and the antiseptic regularity of urban life at the time.

But, then again, lightning does tend to strike out from storm clouds. The Sex Pistols first hit British television a couple of months prior to the single's release, Lydon opening this cataclysmic slot with the battle yell: "Get off your arse!" Thus did Tony Wilson bring them to the nation's prime stage. The band performed to type, mocking and sneering with all the venom of what until then had been more of a capital city confrontation than anything else. Now it was public knowledge – and on telly, of all places. Lydon's red hair matched his torn pink jacket, held together as one garment by safety pins – soon to become one of punk's best-known badges. Jordan Mooney, asked to back up the band with her presence, later remembered the audience sitting motionless, too stunned by what they were witnessing to react.

Following unexpected foul language on national television, the world of the Pistols was blown open. Glory was theirs for the taking. They took it, encouraged by McLaren, who knew a gift horse when he saw one. But the cosy, high finance world of EMI was also blown open, and following an outcry in various safe, right-leaning British newspapers, the label buckled under pressure, dropping the band, even though the record had made the top 40 chart. But their new signings had followed and created controversy through the final month of the year, refusing to lie low, mocking and fighting, including amongst themselves – "Like cats and dogs," as Lydon remarked later. At the packaging plant handling the notorious single a strike was called in protest. There were improvised demos outside gigs. The nation was aflame and the Sex Pistols were the public's target. EMI could not withstand such an onslaught.

In more youthful quarters, the Pistols and their brand of subversion were seen as inspirational. Up and down a tired, bland, trussed-up England, young people gazed in awe and admiration at the vanguard of the new movement. This was something they wanted to be part of… that they *needed* to be part of. They felt the same ennui and anger that their heroes felt. A flame had been put to combustible material. Innumerable punk bands were instigated because of the Sex Pistols and their early television appearances, and not just in London. In Manchester, one of the most significant scenes would soon emerge, spearheaded by Pete Shelley and Howard Devoto.

When the Sex Pistols attempted to travel to a series of gigs in the Netherlands, the chaos of their journey, reported next day in the press, became the last straw for EMI. Harm had been done to their reputation and they could take no more. They dropped the band, albeit honouring the signed contract. The forty thousand pounds that they had handed over was no more.

Already, however, seismic waves were passing through the band members and their manager. Paul Cook behind the drum kit had in earlier days threatened to leave the band because he had a job, and, ironically as it turned out, saw no future for the motley crew. Glen Matlock's position on bass was unstable. He would soon be replaced by a character almost as notorious as John Lydon: Sid Vicious. Steve Jones remained onboard. As for Lydon himself, his insight, intelligence and quick thinking made him realise what potential lay ahead for the band. Publicity was the key, for all that he despised most of what lay before him in the black and white of printed words, and despite his loathing of formal television procedures. His was a stance of rage and confrontation, and it needed to be seen, recognised and acknowledged. It was no accident that his opening line to his soon-to-be adoring fan base was: "Get off your arse!" That omnipresent, enervating, hopeless ennui which he saw on city streets, that miasma of apathy caused by the oppressive weight of the establishment had to be destroyed. The public hardly noticed it, because it was an invisible atmosphere of British culture, occasionally pierced by academics in their university offices, sometimes mentioned by Communists or other political dissenters. Lydon saw a new opening, prised open with his own vituperative lyrics and the three-minute, glorious tirade of *Anarchy In The U.K.* He could not have wished for a better beginning to the campaign.

The single vanished from number 38 on the BMRB's charts. Events were happening at breakneck speed: filthy and furious on ITV, being dropped, finding fans, fuelling a movement, writing more songs. *Anarchy In The U.K.* had set its sights on general British traditions, but there was one target that Brits worshipped more than any, and that was the royal family.

Thus, a new target came into view.

Chapter 7

Denim & Long Black Hair

On Bicentennial Day, 4 July 1976, The Ramones were scheduled on the bill at a sell-out gig at the Roundhouse in London. It was their first date outside America. This was a much anticipated event for some of the upcoming British punk bands, all of whom were still working to get deals, perform their own gigs, acquire more fans and shout out the message. Neither *New Rose* nor *Anarchy In The U.K.* had yet been released and the punk movement was an exciting, though still London-centric scene.

Part of the source of that scene lay across the Pond, not least in New York City, where The Ramones, a.k.a. Da Brudders, had their operational base. When *New Rose* hit the streets in October 1976, the seminal Ramones debut LP, self-titled and released on Sire Records, was already six months out of the starting blocks and attracting much attention. Captain Sensible used to play his bass along with the record, noting to his delight that the music was easy to follow. It was fresh, stripped-down, exciting. Just what he wanted.

Another crucial band of the time, The Ruts, also found inspiration in the sound. The Ramones' album was a league away from what almost everybody younger than their early twenties thought to be a tired, bland, bloated music world. By contrast, The Ramones were simple. A few chords, repeated lyrics, black leather, denim and attitude.

That said, although in America this debut album claimed much music press praise, in Britain the band's name was known only to a comparatively small circle, most of it in the burgeoning punk movement and at the *NME,* where occasional Sex Pistols guitarist Nick Kent and Charles Shaar Murray were enthusiastic fans. To the cognoscenti, therefore, The Ramones were a known quantity. Readers of the music press could become part of a Brudders clique if they wanted to – an exciting place to be. Ironically, the four men comprising The Ramones were all Anglophiles, who had grown up with various classic British groups.

Also on the bill that day were The Flamin' Groovies, while The Stranglers were third on the roster. Almost two thousand young fans packed out the venue, and for all the broad range of talent on show that day it was The Ramones who made the most impact. They played fourteen songs, including *Loudmouth* and *Blitzkrieg Bop,* also *Now I Wanna Sniff Some Glue* and *Judy Is A Punk.* Three encores followed: *Today Your Love Tomorrow The World, Now I Wanna Be A Good Boy* and *Let's Dance.* They invited Marc Bolan on stage. Part of their largesse took the form of model baseball bats promoting the *Blitzkrieg Bop* single, handed out by Joey Ramone – he gave one of them to Gaye Advert, a memento she kept. Their set was a triumph, but, more than that, it was inspirational. This was a gig that galvanised the British movement. As more than one future punk luminary noted, the songs were pretty much over by the time you knew what they were and had the gist of the tune and words. That was a template for the future.

Fans in attendance that night included Rat Scabies of The Damned and The Adverts' Gaye Advert. The Clash and the Sex Pistols were gigging in Sheffield at the time, but caught Da Brudders the night after at Dingwalls for a second sold-out show. Scabies later remarked that seeing The Ramones made him realise that many in his generation were feeling the same anger, leading to the same explosion of incendiary music. In London, surfing a comparatively small scene, he had felt alone. He did not feel that way any longer.

Blitzkrieg Bop came out in February 1976, and from the beginning was a punk inspiration in Britain. Written by the band's drummer Tommy with additions by bassist Dee Dee, its simple chord scheme, memorable tune and easy lyrics turned it into a classic, though at the time that was little recognised. The band were as good as unknown beyond their home city, and knew next to nothing about the British scene. Punk rock was an American thing, a street thing, a Ramones thing. That a parallel movement existed in nascent form in, of all places, England was a considerable surprise to them.

Their stock in trade was youthful energy, fast pace, stripped back songs, and a commitment to ending a song well before it overstayed its welcome. Not for them the jazz enigma of Steely Dan or the harmonically sophisticated country sound of the Eagles. They were a street band in denim and black leather, their fringes meeting their eyebrows. They could play their instruments well enough, but that did not matter. What *did* matter was the energy, the relatable lyrics, the sense of catering for an audience who had transistor radios not hi-fi sets. Theirs, indeed, was a lo-fi agenda.

Blitzkrieg Bop was the first song on their debut album, yet more than that it opened with a snatched chant – *Hey! Ho! Let's go!* – which would resonate down the decades. Released on 45 as *The Blitzkrieg Bop!* the song was about gig experiences, telling a simple tale of street kids going out for the night. Its iconic opening was half pinched from a Bay City Rollers song with a similar line in chants, and it catered for Joey's pop leanings, for Tommy's writing chops, and for Dee Dee's earthy bass.

Though they had no intention of copying the Phil Spector wall of sound, their thrashing guitars and bass thrum did give the song a similar feel, powerful and catchy. It was the perfect LP opener.

In Britain, the band began to get known and admired amongst members of punk's inner circle, and by the time their second album *Leave Home* was released it scraped the bottom of the U.K. charts, hitting number 45 – not bad for January 1977, when punk had only just hit the headlines. Things were evolving fast.

The Ramones' use of the term punk rock in their classic *Sheena Is A Punk Rocker* also made waves in Britain. Although this song appeared a few months after punk's notoriety exploded into the public consciousness, its popularity (it reached number 22 in the singles charts), and use of the term helped various elements of the movement coalesce still further. The 45 was released in May 1977 in Britain, when all punk's elements of notoriety, youth appeal and rebellion were fixed into a distinctive press-fuelled image. Although The Ramones had their own look, dissimilar from the classic British punk fashion, they were still worthy of respect.

Written by front man Joey Ramone, the song, with its catchy melody and easy lyrics, was both a hit and an inspiration. Joey Ramone wrote it as a rebellion song, imagining how the graphic novel character Sheena Queen of the Jungle might react as she arrived in the so-called civilised world. His was a primal sound, stripped back to the basics of rock. The punk rock of the song was the movement making headlines, inspiring a generation of angry, buttoned-down youth. It was very nearly an anthem.

Well the kids are all hopped up and ready to go ... But she just couldn't stay, she had to break away... Then the chorus, repeated, repeated, repeated: *Sheena is a punk rocker...* The simplicity of these lyrics, when seen in printed form, belies their considerable influence. They are almost shockingly sparse. And the single was not just popular amongst record buying fans; the *NME* placed it in fifth position in their 1977 list of the year's best, further cementing its reputation. Since then its renown has been assured. Punk rock, and Sheena who was a punk rocker, were both in town. This was a new movement, a new momentum, winding itself up like a tornado then releasing its energy in storm form. As some writers of the movement observed, punk was not so much a primitive music, it was a *primal* music.

Moreover, as The Ramones themselves pointed out, part of their ethos was that they could not play their instruments well. But that *didn't matter.* What mattered was attitude, giving the fans a show, making a racket, annoying parents. Punk, epitomised by The Ramones and their three chord classics, was a *democratising* movement. The Ramones at the Roundhouse – a rough and ready venue at the time – and at Dingwalls the night afterwards gave permission for young people to take up an unfamiliar object, a musical instrument, learn the basics, then get out there and tell their truth. It was an empowering force, a rejection of dexterity, a snub to virtuosity: a roots movement.

By the time all this was underway, the band themselves were back in New York. They only found out what they had achieved later on.

Hal Harries worked for many years as a member of the bar staff and front of house at the Rainbow Theatre in Finsbury Park. A regular reader of the *NME* and a big music fan, he observed the sharp divide between times before punk and times afterward.

> *Before punk, I used to see a lot of showmanship at the Rainbow – exhibitionist musicians and fifteen-minute drum solos. But the arrival of punk was a sharp dividing line between it and what went before. There was no blur. The whole atmosphere of the venue changed when punk bands played – a lot more anarchic. It was always more riotous – not necessarily more*

violent, but more rumbustious. It was a different kind of energy for punk bands. Although the layout of the venue meant it was not so conducive to gobbing, there was more beer being chucked! It was crazy, though without being threatening.

He detected a difference between the American version of punk and the British version inspired by that New York scene.

The British punk vibe was different to the American version. American bands seemed more managed and slicker. The British punk bands were more chaotic and crazy – more unstructured. With American bands it seemed more about the showmanship, even for the more "down to earth" bands like The Ramones. The Brits were more chaotic, less showy. It was a different, madder energy.

Chapter 8

"You Dirty Fucker!"

Freddie Mercury did not like going to the dentist. It was this element of the rock star's life that led to the Sex Pistols acquiring the glorious notoriety for which overnight they became famous.

At the time, many television personalities – and indeed radio DJs – were treated as minor gods by the brown-nosers of the broadcast media, and Bill Grundy, journalist, was one such. He was not used to being mocked, messed around or having disrespect dished out in his direction. Legend has it that he and at least one Sex Pistols band member were drunk prior to the 1 December 1976 show, but Glen Matlock was not so sure in its aftermath. Anyway, Grundy came from a working environment where a liquid lunch was normal; he could take his liquor. His Thames Television show was guaranteed good publicity for bands, so when EMI discovered that Mercury, their original guest, *was* visiting the dentist, they struggled to find a replacement for that edition of the show.

They needed to offer somebody. Their new signings would have to do.

Lydon at least of the quartet felt patronised as the live broadcast began. Quick-witted, perceptive and resentful, he clocked Grundy's manner from the outset of what turned out to be a chaotic ninety seconds. The band sat at ease in their chairs, Lydon to the right, then Jones, Matlock and Cook. Grundy sat to their left, beaming at the camera. Behind the band stood Siouxsie Sioux, Steve Severin, Simon Barker and Simone, looking either uncomfortable or baffled.

What happened next soon achieved the status of legend. Grundy first spoke to camera, explaining that the new breed were punk rockers, the new craze. With him were a group of them called the Sex Pistols; and he felt surrounded. At this point, film of the band playing live was shown, with Jones interrupting Grundy reading the autocue. A barney then developed between Grundy and Matlock as the matter of the forty thousand pounds advance was discussed, Grundy questioning the band's ethics then suggesting they were not a serious proposition. Beethoven, Mozart, Bach and Brahms had all died, he pointed out.

At this point, Lydon began muttering. Grundy asked him what he was saying, to which Lydon replied that such composers were their heroes, and wonderful people. With obvious sarcasm, he said: *They really turn us on.* A swear word followed. Grundy caught it at once, goading Lydon into repeating it. Lydon accepted the challenge: *Shit.*

But Grundy did not look particularly bothered by any of this. In mockery he said how the band frightened him to death, then, as if bored, he turned his attention to Siouxsie Sioux: *Are you worried, or are you just enjoying yourself?*

Siouxsie even then was no shrinking violet nineteen-year-old overawed by being on television. She replied that she was enjoying myself. Grundy, checking, explained that was what he thought she was doing. Yet Siouxsie had a devastating response to Grundy's dead-eyed flattery. I always wanted to meet you, she told him. Grundy, surprised, wanted to be sure, and when Siouxsie confirmed this, he told her they should meet afterwards. Steve Jones had to respond to that: *You dirty sod. You dirty old man!*

Even this foul-mouthed attack failed to affect Grundy. He mocked Jones, calling him Chief, then telling him to say something outrageous in the remaining five seconds. Jones promptly accepted. Grundy was a dirty bastard, a dirty fucker and a fucking rotter. Jones by contrast was, according to Grundy, just a clever boy. But now Grundy's time was up; and he knew he had been bested. Telling the Pistols that he hoped never to see them again, he signed off. As the signature tune played out and the credits rolled he grinned and muttered: *Oh shit.* He knew he was in trouble.

As if this incident by itself was not enough, investigations undertaken much later by the music press discovered an extraordinary fact. By the time the Pistols and those members of the Bromley Contingent (including Siouxsie Sioux) behind them on set had been led by producer Martin Lucas to the green room, the Thames Television offices were being deluged with phone calls from shocked and outraged viewers. When the phone answering system exceeded its call limit, the unanswered calls were sent down to the green room, where the Pistols and their cohort began answering. Thus, even more verbal outrage was generated.

The quartet, rehearsing for their upcoming Anarchy Tour, had not even wanted to do this broadcast interview, Matlock later suggesting that they had been given their orders by EMI. When a lengthy limousine drove up to transport them to the television studio they were even more annoyed. No punk, least of all the Sex Pistols, should be seen travelling in a vehicle like that. At length, with Malcolm McLaren threatening to dock their wages, they assented, piling in irritation into the luxury vehicle before heading off for the interview.

Warnings about foul language proffered by lesser employees at Thames Television were ignored as it became clear who Mercury's replacement would be. And although Grundy opened his chat by remarking that the band were more drunk than he was, that seems upon viewing of the video tape to be unlikely. He just had no idea who he was dealing with, enjoyed a terrific opinion of himself, and did not see the oncoming car crash.

It was his arrogance that led to him being vexed by Jones mimicking him as he read the autocue. Besides, he was middle aged, and the youths in front of him looked only just out of school; he saw them as unclean, undeserving children. He dismissed them, punk, and the whole ethic of the movement before anyone spoke a word. Lydon grasped all that just by looking around. Steve Jones, perhaps more drunk than the others, had stopped caring about the interview and its consequences hours before. Siouxsie Sioux, bopping in faux-happy style, also mocked Grundy and the whole set-up. He retaliated, and everything went downhill from there. This was not an interview any more, it was a tussle to see who could outperform the other. It was verbal jousting. Yet while Grundy had television experience, what the Pistols had far outweighed it. *They* did not care. *They* had John Lydon and Steve Jones. The establishment in all its forms was the enemy. Respect would not be given to those who wanted it purely as a consequence of their social position.

Almost fifty years on, the Grundy incident seems trivial, even inconsequential. If it happened today nobody would take the slightest notice. The difference in 1976 was entrenched British cultural values.

Bill Grundy and the edifice of Thames Television – which stood as a mere David to the Goliath of the BBC – were a manifestation of something far older, more tenacious, and more self-serving than any mere television company. Grundy was in effect a scion of the establishment, a vector of tradition, of the good old British way of doing things. He faced the first modern home-grown cultural movement ever to pitch up at the ivory towers of London Town. Although punk had been championed by the music press, with the Sex Pistols, The Damned, The Clash and The Stranglers all featuring frequently in their ink-stained rags, mainstream media, especially television, knew nothing of the danger milling around their ankles. Now those ankles, protected by socks from Saville Row, were being bitten.

Thames memos and notes released later show that studio producer Mike Housego saw the potential for trouble, but as getting a film package ready took time, and because clearing the studio floor could have provoked worse trouble, he decided he had to let the interview continue. Grundy, hearing Housego's voice in his earpiece, was told to chill, but by then it was too late. Grundy wanted to prove that the band were oafs, that they were childish, that no good would come from mere street yobs. As the interview descended into chaos, he openly provoked the band into uttering profanities: *Go on, you've another five seconds, say something outrageous.* So they did. They had necked a few beers and were having a laugh. It was what they did – their style, their way. This was a clash of cultures, fuelled by arrogance from the traditional side and mockery from the underdogs. It could only end one way.

That way became apparent next morning. Everyone of a certain age remembers the classic Daily Mirror headline: *The Filth And The Fury.*

Malcolm McLaren later tried to claim that he was delighted at the publicity the band had acquired in just a minute and a half, but in fact he was bricking it. Even he, McLaren the raconteur turned punk Situationist, was in part beholden to the overriding attitude of the time, that behaviour, language and comportment were all important to the British way of doing things. Even he did not quite realise what combustible materials had been assembled in the years leading up to the punk explosion. He expected disaster; and, at the outset, it did look like the Daily Mirror had summarised a disaster in just five words.

Yet it was no catastrophe. Though it led to the hounding of the Sex Pistols and many others of the punk movement as the enemy the British people loved to hate, it also opened those floodgates of fury which had been locked shut by the nation's pleasant, decent, understated way of doing things. Punk was not nice, and did not want to be. Punk had no intention of being decent. Punk could never be understated. These were real feelings bubbling up: resentment, anger, scorn, sardonic mockery. John Lydon, that brilliant wit, encapsulated those feelings within the band. The Sex Pistols encapsulated those feelings within the movement. Other bands would deal with the political side of the movement, with social norms and transgression, with the sheer joy of being young and loathing your parents, but the Sex Pistols were the manifestation of that fury inside young, disenfranchised people during the middle of the 1970s.

What the Sex Pistols did "wrong" on that day was to break an unwritten rule. The British are good at making those. However, they have to be part of the establishment to know them all. The rule the Sex Pistols broke was that requiring *deference.* British society worked – and still works – by having an elite at the top who have not earned their place and who are deemed worthy of respect merely because of that position. Though that is obvious, especially to those at the bottom of the heap, the unwritten rule of deference is subtle and applies to all public forms, even ones nominally aimed at the lower classes. Swearing on live television and manifestly not caring one jot for the television presenter in front of them or the consequences of their actions marked the Pistols as *outsiders.* They came from *elsewhere,* and needed to be treated as such, at first by Grundy, then by the rest of the simpering, flag-waving nation.

In later years, having had his hand slapped, Grundy claimed that he had intentionally confronted the band because of the mismatch between their actions and their ethics – the squandered £40,000 for instance. The truth or otherwise of that statement is irrelevant. What matters is that the social milieu in which at the time and afterwards he set the incident was one of conflict between the underclasses and the privileged; and he felt he was one of the privileged. It was them against us. He would prove the Sex Pistols and their hangers-on were street yobs, or, at least, say afterwards that was what he was doing. Class conflict was an unspoken assumption in his dealings with the band and through the media furore which followed. Swearing, mocking and being sarcastic were un-British activities.

The Bill Grundy incident and its aftermath happened for the same reason that the Goon Show was almost axed by the BBC, then to be saved by its internal defender, John Snagge. The one thing the British establishment hates is not being taken seriously. It is a point of ironic cultural interest that one face of that establishment, lovely "Aunty Beeb," managed to propel The Goons, TW3 and Monty Python amongst others into national prominence. Yet even Spike Milligan's anarchy was comparatively safe, because it was absurdist and because it was funny. The Sex Pistols were genuinely dangerous. Their music was neither absurd nor funny. It was something to be frightened of.

Chapter 9

The Look

Jordan Mooney was the dancer dressed in an Anarchy T shirt standing behind the Sex Pistols on their television debut *So It Goes,* the band having been brought in by Tony Wilson, who was always on the lookout for new talent. Her outfit also included a swastika armband, which, despite requests, Mooney refused to remove. Thus was another seminal moment in punk's history marked, albeit, at the time, by only a few astonished viewers.

Mooney became one of punk's defining individuals, and is credited with devising a lot of what morphed into the punk look. Yet beside her in the King's Road SEX fashion boutique stood two of punk's titans, Malcolm McLaren and Vivienne Westwood, overshadowing her, except perhaps in the eyes of the members of the still small clique who would become punk rock's early core. It was Westwood who would receive much of the credit for creating the various elements of punk fashion, yet Mooney played as important a role.

She was not a natural rebel. She felt herself to be an artist, an individualist, a rider of waves crashing into the stranger shores of British subculture. She had no time for normality and fitting in. Though her look was marked by outré hair styling, provocative clothes and wild make-up, the rebellious character of the style was less important than the fact that *she* was doing it. She was being herself. Punk, at the very beginning, was an ethic of individual freedom in search of true identity. Dave Vanian wore winklepickers in the early days for the same reason Mooney wore latex: that was how they wished to look. It was *their* look. End of.

That is not to say she did not enjoy parading her fashion choices. One famous story has her banished to a first-class train carriage so that London's delicate railway commuters would not be offended when they clapped eyes on her. It is a mark of the twisted, repressed social mores of the time that such an occurrence could happen, that public nuisance in the eyes of the wielders of traditional power – even *railway* employees, for goodness' sake – could be deemed so reprehensible. Yet reprehensible it was deemed. Mooney thought little of all this fuss. She did not care about public opinion. Anyway, she felt comfortable in her clothes.

There was another aspect to this, however, for which punk became an unexpected vector. Part of the democratising effect of the movement was to bring women, especially young women, into the public arena, a place dominated by men since time began. Britain was as righteous a patriarchal state as any other, and it did not like mere women getting uppity by designing their own fashion statements. This would have major repercussions later, for bands such as The Slits.

When Mooney came across McLaren and Westwood in the SEX fashion shop, something clicked in her mind. Having changed her name early in her teenage years – a common way of redefining identity in the face of discomfort – she felt that in SEX her true self had found a real home. There, she fitted. There, the customers were more like her. Some felt a sense of unease inside the premises, with its dark aura and graffiti-spattered walls, but not her.

The manager Michael Collins hired her as a shop assistant (Westwood found that out later). In the early days she met the New York Dolls and many other notables, the shop acting as a focus for gathering punk discontent. Yet it was far from being just a shop. This place had an ethic, a reason for existing, one determined and managed by the central trio: Mooney, McLaren and Westwood. They were not there simply to sell clothes and count their takings at the end of the day, they would instigate intense conversations with their customers, finding out why they had visited, what they were like as individuals, and what they really wanted. It was a fashion dialectic mediated by the trio, sourced in the outré clothes, concluding with a purchase only if everyone was satisfied with that outcome. SEX and its ethic was a kind of ritual, a deep meaning self-created, which was about more than merely clothes and making money. SEX was not about veneers; it was the real thing.

Mooney sensed beauty in the garments she was selling. She was matching plumage with inner self, and it felt like a devotional act – her vocation, her *calling*. She was an artist in fabric, spreading her message to sincere converts only. Selling a cobweb sweater or a latex skirt was to her an act imbued with meaning. Such garments could not therefore be passed on to poseurs who had the money but lacked the substance. That rigour in sales technique gave her something of a reputation as dark and aloof, but the truth was more nuanced. She would sometimes help customers lacking funds, for instance. She was not all about controlling the dialectic.

Moreover, she recognised that Vivienne Westwood had a brilliance for fashion design.

After Westwood met McLaren, she dissolved her marriage to Derek Westwood and moved with McLaren to a place in Balham. Already a designer of jewellery, she moved into fashion with McLaren at her side, and in due course the Sex Pistols and the shop's other customers began to become more visible as punk standard bearers. Indeed, in punk, Westwood recognised something which made her an evangelist for the nascent movement. A working-class girl from Cheshire, she saw in the new energy and bands an opportunity to upset the well-oiled cogs of traditional British values. This was a cultural force she could get behind, that she could support, and even facilitate with shocking new looks.

The various components of the punk look came together as the shop developed, their customer base improved and became more of a coherent scene, and Westwood and McLaren progressed with designs and accessories. They usually worked in collaboration, but Westwood had her own interests and predilections, using historical research as a source as well as her own imagination. She also found joy in the increasing appearance and acceptance of women in the punk movement, something occurring in parallel with a new wave of feminism spearheaded by iconic figures – Germaine Greer – and by important academics – Kate Millett and Eva Figes not least. She was a fluid experimentalist, a true original.

Many of the garments, looks and accessories available in SEX were deliberately intended to upset the status quo. Seventies Britain was a buttoned-up, beige, boring place to live for many of its adolescents, and both Westwood and McLaren realised they could inspire young people and provoke traditionalists by emphasising fetish gear and S&M styles, which for the tittering, simpering masses were usually located in Soho establishments. But not anymore. SEX brought that subculture – so embarrassing to the

British, so damned *difficult* – onto a main road in London. Theirs was a fierce stance, not the guffawing, childish attitude of a middle class for whom even the word sex was naughty. Westwood and McLaren both observed a too-comfortable majority in their home country. They wanted to bring some grit into life. Conformity was anathema to them.

In 1976 the boutique took another new name, metamorphosing into Seditionaries: Clothes For Heroes. Now Westwood was working with new types of fabric, resulting in a range of clothes that epitomised the punk movement: bondage trousers, cobweb jumpers with underwear visible beneath, ripped T shirts, and straps – lots of straps. She also devised a look worn by John Lydon in some of his early performances, long-sleeved tops made of muslin, all of them emblazoned with screen print designs. These, worn by the sneering, scowling Lydon, made him look as if he had emerged from the nearest sanitorium. Such designs were so different from the high street norm they became instant punk statements, soon visible on the streets of every British city.

In due course, as punk, with the same inevitability of the hippie movement the previous decade, blew out its own storm and mutated into New Wave and post-punk, Westwood became disillusioned with the lack of rigour in the movement. She too moved on to other fashions.

The origin of that iconic punk accessory the safety pin is shrouded in mystery, likely never to be unmasked. One hypothesis has its origin with Richard Hell and the Voidoids, a New York band aligned to the proto-punk movement. Hell would rip his clothes and pin them back together again, a style observed by Malcolm McLaren when he flew across the Atlantic to check out various bands. Hell also had the omnidirectional spiked hair look that would soon end up on John Lydon and many others. McLaren could easily have been the vector of that look. Lydon himself, however, when questioned about the safety pins he wore in his T shirt at the beginning of punk, merely remarked that he needed something to hold his disintegrating garments together. For him, the safety pin was a utilitarian object.

Whatever the origin, the combined forces of the Pistols, Westwood and McLaren, and various elements of chance and imitation caused the safety pin to achieve iconic status. It was also easy to obtain and cheap, virtues recommending it to those skint outsiders following the punk movement.

That Westwood accentuated its use was one factor in its popularity, but it also had shock value when used to pierce skin. That shock was the perfect vehicle for punk's ethic of confrontation and the caustic rejection of tradition.

The safety pin also symbolised the D.I.Y. attitude of the movement. High street fashion was for the middle classes, and had been created by corporations. Such clothes were for sheep. Punk said: get something, write on it with a big marker pen, then rough it up. Safety pins will hold it together. Such styles were statements of rejection as well as nonconformity.

As for the A-in-the-circle which epitomised the punk ethos of anarchy, that was an older symbol acquired and repurposed by the movement. Its earliest attested use goes back as far as the middle of the nineteenth century, in Spanish documents intended to fight capitalist exploitation – even then it was a working-class symbol. Anarchy became a concept in many political theatres as that century morphed into the twentieth, with an A inside an O the often utilised symbol.

Punk's use of A-in-O brought it to a much wider audience, fuelled by modern visual media. It signified damage to tradition: to property, to morals, to the middle and upper classes. It became a graffiti icon sprayed on ten thousand walls. Soon it appeared in fanzines and on clothes, made to appear rougher and angrier by making the A too big for the O. This was a true symbol of the movement.

Punk vinyl cover designs also broke through traditional styles. Many album covers from the mid-seventies period defied tradition and even commercial common sense in a manner guaranteed to cause a stir. But that was the point. Punk bands had new products to sell. Richard Hell and the Voidoids' *Blank Generation* album featured the man himself, shirt wide open on the front cover, with 'You Make Me —' tattooed on his chest; an image both compelling and disquieting. The Damned meanwhile opted for the gunk and lunacy of themselves covered in scrumptious cream, an image also disquieting, albeit funny, and unforgettable – totally in character. Their label Stiff Records however had their own ideas about the back cover, early editions of which featured Eddie & the Hot Rods, a publicity stunt by the wily label owners, though they changed it soon afterwards to a photo of the band playing at the Roxy Club. As early as 1976, The Ramones pulled off an iconic grubby black and white photograph of themselves that became much imitated in punk circles, and beyond. The debut LP by The Clash was also a grainy black and white photograph, its surrounds in rough green and orange suggesting new music in a new direction. *Pure Mania* by The Vibrators, while more of a stylised image, still relied on black and white and a huge V suggesting two fingers.

Singles were just as susceptible to the new design ethic. *The Day The World Turned Day-Glo* by X-Ray Spex came housed in a livid sleeve hued green and red, its design scrawled in places, its typography suggesting haste. It stood out a mile. *Blitzkrieg Bop,* the inspirational Ramones song, came in a graphic novel sleeve, using photographs and hand-written text that *Sniffin' Glue* fanzine would echo the following year. Its design was a conceptual anti-salute to the carefully airbrushed images and posed photographs of single releases from earlier years. Montage, meanwhile, was not only used by Jamie Reid of Sex Pistols fame. Linder Sterling provided the unforgettable image for Buzzcocks' *Orgasm Addict* release, which strayed into controversial territory while just about remaining within decent bounds. The colour palette was bright, even harsh, but the combined sarcasm and humour of the image showed traditional designers that new forms were required for this new music. *Nobody's Scared* by Subway Sect also took the monochrome route, its stark image a train on London's underground, the band's name presented as if graffiti on the wall (rather like the debut Jam album *In The City* from '77). The Damned took their destructive streak to its logical conclusion by presenting their debut 45 in a sleeve showing a fragmented bass drum. It said so much with so little: chaos, disorder, demolition. *Problem Child* the following year was a monochrome cut-up of the band with newspaper text, while *Stretcher Case Baby* was even more macabre, riffing on a Salvador Dali skull image and using full gothic text. The debut Eater single, *Outside View,* was also monochrome, presenting the young band as if behind prison bars, while their debut album had a creepy close-up of an ant.

Not all these designs were shocking, but in the context of what had appeared before they were at least striking. A new design ethic was appearing, with its own torn and spiky typography and its own rough 'n' ready ethos. Gritty black and white took over from sumptuous colour – a reaction against the perceived luxury and aloofness of the groups that punk bands wanted to separate themselves from. Some of these early punk designs had the intent of presenting something vibrant, chaotic and out of control, but in some cases the look was formed more by necessity than design. Those bands manufacturing their own vinyl releases could not afford graphic designer prices, their only other option using what lay around them: found images, newspapers and magazines, rough and ready photography, all of which suggested menace, excitement, change. Rebellion and revolution were in the air, and cover design was one way to invoke that sea change in the British music scene.

Where did the plastic fashion look come from? Captain Sensible stuck to his white plastic sunglasses once he realised they were making him stand out, but that was far from the only manifestation of plastic in punk fashion.

Punks used fashion choices to emphasise their political stance as well as their wish to discard the establishment and oppose its values, which they saw as indicative of the conservatism and elitism of British society – the monarchy and the old boys' network of politics in particular. God save the Queen? No. Fashion of all sorts came to their aid, and not just T shirts. The ragged look, the distressed look, the use of text and subverted images all counted. These were ways of opposing, of standing apart from older people, of settling identity and of finding like-minded friends. Nothing helped as much in seeking new acquaintances as an *Anarchy* T shirt or a green dyed spiky haircut. And this was not just about dressing up for effect, though, in later years, some punks became tourist destinations as they preened themselves in the centre of London. Punk was about seeing the truth, escaping your prison cell, following your own road. Punk fashion was a way of taking control of your life, of moving from passive to active. It was, in fact, a statement of anti-fashion, delivered with delicious irony in the way only the British know how to do.

Plastic, before becoming more prevalent as the seventies progressed on the back of commercial profits, was viewed at first as a novelty. A material that had never been used to any great extent in fashion, its ubiquity and shock value when used in an unfamiliar context made it attractive to early punks. But its inexpensiveness was also important. This material was not silk or linen. It could be appropriated for garments at little cost.

For Vivienne Westwood, at the time relatively unknown and able to experiment with little constraint, plastic allowed her designs both to stand out and be affordable. She considered the Sex Pistols to be living models for her clothes, who merely by heading out into town would market her look, her ethos and her mythology. That mythology would soon become her legend. By then, however, she had tired of street nihilism, and moved onward and upwards.

Plastic did not look like a fashion material in ways which at the time were considered shocking. By the mid-1970s, adolescent girls had been identified by big business as a critical market, whose combination of pester power and disposable cash, they knew, would make them rich. More importantly, that market would never diminish, giving them the financial stability these capitalist exploiters craved. But this tradition of middle-class security, money and choice was exactly what punks mocked or opposed. So it was that the black bin bag, utilitarian and utterly without redeeming fashion credentials, became a totem of the early punks. It epitomised their scorn of corporate manipulation, of conservative design, of the sort of twee marketing which made them want to retch. It was perfect: cheap, incongruous, and as far away from the catwalk as it was possible to be.

When Debbie Harry wore a bin bag jacket to sing *Atomic* on *Top Of The Pops* in 1980, she was a couple of years behind trend. Yet her appearance was just as shocking on television as it had been on the streets of London a couple of years earlier. Bin bag plastic had *arrived*. Moreover, it had arrived for young *women*, who prior to punk had faced little choice and a lot of strictures when making the move from child to adult. Young women were supposed to look good in the *traditional* way. Adopting plastic and the bin bag look was as sarcastic a response as could be imagined in the late 1970s, and traditional men were not used to that.

Another critical aspect of the cheapness of plastic as a fashion material was that it could be manipulated at home, with not much more than pinking shears and high-quality needles required. That move between fashion delivered to young people via shops, and fashion created in the bedrooms and on the kitchen tables of houses by young people themselves was an essential part of punk's ethos. It meant individualism. It meant unique looks.

It was a move from passive to active – the critical core of punk's manifesto. D.I.Y. wherever possible.

The British origin of the signature punk hair style the mohican is shrouded in mystery. Although much is known about those Native American peoples who wore similar styles, the reason for punk rockers taking it up remains obscure. Even the commonly accepted name is a misnomer, since the Mohawk tribe in the region now occupied by New York technically wore scalp locks, in which a strip of hair, often decorated, was left running down from the crown of the head. In fact it was the Pawnee people, resident in the state now called Nebraska, who sported a style more akin to the classic punk mohican.

Whatever the truth, British punks took up the mohican with alacrity, expanding its possibilities as the 1970s ended with a variety of substances which allowed lengthy sections of hair to defy gravity. The punk mohican was a raised line of hair treated with gel or similar products to make it stand up into a cockscomb. Hair dye – or dyes for a really eye-catching effect – improved the style further. Variations included twin lines of hair bunched up into spikes that would have been impressive on a triceratops dinosaur.

What made punk fashion even more shocking to the middle-class baby boomers of seventies Britain was that *women* also adopted the mohican. This development verged on transgressive, since, at a time when feminism was a mocked and suppressed campaign, women were expected to conform to all male imposed norms, one of which was that their hair should be long and flowing – the symbol of a sexuality that men demanded they embody. But young punk women were having none of that. Moreover, as Viv Albertine remarked, punk was the only time outspoken women could say what was on their minds and still fit in with everyone else. Women were supposed to fit in, yes; but with patriarchal norms. That was what men wanted. To rebel meant to take symbols emphasised by male-dominated culture and subvert them, women's hair being perfect in that regard. For a woman to sport a really striking mohican therefore was to declare that patriarchy was under attack. It was a sign of the times.

Early punk hairstyles were usually dramatic. The classic mohican was little seen in Britain in the earliest days, with spikes, as modelled by John Lydon and Sid Vicious, being more common examples. Live fast and burn out punk originals The Maniacs flirted with the style. Susan Lucas, known to the nascent London movement as Soo Catwoman, wore a twinned mohican raised up at the sides of her head. With her distressed, cut-up fashion choices she was a superb embodiment of what young punk women could aspire to in their fight to be authentic to their own wishes. A regular on the scene and a friend to the Sex Pistols, her choice to shave the crown of her head was particularly striking, shaving off the hair of a woman being for decades a symbol of female degradation. Meanwhile, as punk began to mutate into post-punk and New Wave, a Scottish band called The Exploited appeared carrying the punk torch, with Wattie Buchan, their vocalist, sporting a fine mohican. Legend has it that he was influenced by Darby Crash of American punks The Germs, whose mohican was a stylish black cockscomb.

Whatever their historical origins, what the mohican, the spiked style, and the range of dayglo dyes used by punks to transform their hair represented was rebellion. It was a clear sign of the intent to disregard stuffy, traditional, restrictive social mores. It was a declaration; a challenge. Hair in human culture has always been critical in the representation of self, of identity and of status. Punk hair styles demolished the British standard and replaced it with something new, something *authentic.* Theirs was an outsider chic, designed to shock, but also intended to inform the establishment of the new manifesto. To other punks, the mohican was a symbol of belonging, that profound human need to be one with individuals who share a world view. Punks wanted to mobilise against authority, as do all downtrodden people, but they also wanted to act en masse. This was a *social* movement as much as a musical one.

Chapter 10

Glue Sniffin'

Mark Perry was a bank clerk before he became a punk luminary, instigator of the fanzine *Sniffin' Glue,* then musical explorer in his band Alternative TV. *Sniffin' Glue* – or *Sniffin' Glue and Other Rock 'N' Roll Habits* to give it its full name – was a pioneer of self-publishing, undertaken through photocopying and fat nib marker pens. A founding publication of the punk movement, its idiosyncratic appearance, disregard for grammar and spelling, and sheer enthusiasm made it essential reading for punks in the early days.

Perry had long hair and went to Led Zeppelin concerts before the punk bug bit him. A massive rock fan, he enjoyed much of the scene during the mid-1970s, acts such as Lynyrd Skynyrd and Neil Young from America, and the home-grown Who amongst others. But Zep, not least John Bonham's half hour drum solo, and then Yes performing excerpts from *Tales From Topographic Oceans,* began to make concert-going a tad stale. Perry started to feel uncomfortable and disillusioned, separated from huge bands in huge venues. Even Dr Feelgood at the Reading Festival did not do it for him. Bands in those days were either incomprehensible or distant. Perry needed change. He felt it as a distant, subconscious warning that something in his musical life was amiss. He wanted something *real.*

Prog rock was sometimes entertaining, but it felt bloated. Glam was escapism and could be twee. Pub rock was often shite.

Moreover, although Labour were in power, the perceived dominance of the unions, combined with events such as the dustbin men's strike and resulting litter-filled streets, made Britain feel fragmented, tired and grim. Perry observed this, as did thousands of his peers. His bank job seemed like a prison sentence – he loathed it. The money he earned was real enough, but it was not *real.* Not street real, anyway.

Gigs and music were his form of escape. He read the *NME,* and through its pages discovered the New York scene, especially bands like The Ramones and venues such as CBGB's. It was because of a review of The Ramones' debut LP by the *NME*'s Nick Kent that he made the effort to buy the album on import, before it was even out in Britain. Listening to it changed his life. This was rock music in the vein of Dr Feelgood, but it was way more exciting and had ten times the attitude. It felt fresh and sounded amazing. Perry was hooked.

When The Ramones played their now legendary gig at the Roundhouse in London, Perry was there. He soaked up the atmosphere. He was inspired. This was the shot of adrenalin he had needed, served up by American three-minute song merchants. No frills, no solos, just words and music.

That gig inspired Perry to put together the first edition of his fanzine. Within a week, *Sniffin' Glue* issue 1 was finished.

Yet even after he had finished it he still felt like an outsider. Not a member of punk's inner circle, he felt alone in his desire to be part of the movement. Though he knew the name Sex Pistols, knew Nick Kent's work in the *NME,* and read reviews avidly, he thought the punk scene was more American than British. Soon, however, he started to meet the members of that inner circle, not least because *Sniffin' Glue* began to get known. He met Caroline Coon of *Melody Maker* and Jonh Ingham of *Sounds,* then started receiving invites for gigs – Eddie and the Hot Rods, the Sex Pistols, and many more. Because Coon, Ingham and others of the music press rated him, he became part of the press pack, going backstage after gigs and generally having a whale of a time. The Rock On record shop in Soho carried his fanzine, and soon others were talking about Mark Perry from *Sniffin' Glue.* He was on the inside, at last.

The fanzine took its name from the Ramones belter *Now I Wanna Sniff Some Glue.* It was published monthly from July 1976, but only lasted a year. Perry was not the only writer, and some of his contributors, notably Danny Baker, later became famous in other areas.

Perry paid little attention to the finer details of writing. What mattered was the vibe and attitude. Besides, until the Bill Grundy detonation on ITV, the mass media paid virtually no attention to the punk movement – an almost year-long media blackout. Perry's fanzine, the first of its kind, was therefore a vital source of information, reviews and photos of what was happening in London, alongside the established music press. That music press, in turn, reviewed the fanzine; and they liked it. Yet the scene in those early days was tiny. Perry would be invited to the 100 Club and there meet notables such as Vivienne Westwood and Malcolm McLaren, names now synonymous with style and flair. It all felt so easy, so natural. He loved punk and punk loved his 'zine.

Fifty copies would be reproduced in the early months, though fame and an ever-increasing readership led to the final copy circulation (featuring a flexi-disc by the just formed Alternative TV) of fifteen thousand. Feedback was critical to Perry. He knew the heart of the fanzine was its breathless, uncompromising style: hand-written titles done with a pen, ragged edges and wobbly lines, plenty of street language. Even the *NME* followed rules of grammar and spelling. In comparison, Perry's publication was a cry from the street itself.

Above all, what *Sniffin' Glue* represented was the D.I.Y. ethic, crucial to the way punk fuelled and replicated itself. The rock groups Perry was seeing in 1975 were behemoths on the horizon, making very loud music at a very long range. That disconnect was dangerous. Punks did everything themselves. The record sellers at Rock On, informing him that there was no such thing as a punk fanzine, told him to go out and do one himself. So he did.

Following his experiences at his first Sex Pistols gig, Perry felt energised in a way he never had before. The first issue of his fanzine had been something of an experiment, put together on adrenalin alone, but the second issue featured some of the central punk bands: the Pistols and the Damned. And he was getting known, he was being recognised. This sense of belonging to something underground, thrilling, transgressive and full of relevance made him feel connected to music in a way John Bonham's thirty-minute drum solo had not. Punk had something to say. *He* had something to say. They were not going to sit on their arses and be complacent. It was all about living in straitened circumstances, often on the dole, usually in council houses, and being ignored or trampled on. Moreover, through luck and the small size of the movement, he had become part of the action.

The long hair went and the clothes changed. He started pogoing with the rest of them at the front of gig audiences. He was a changed man. This was *living.*

Perry soon became an insightful observer of the undercurrents of the punk scene. Recognising that it was about individuals – often outsiders – trying to express themselves, to find an authentic identity, he grasped that a loathing of past music forms was something of a distraction. He saw a link between the counterculture of the hippy movement and the social rejection of punks, albeit that such rejection took an artistic form. But punk rock did have a philosophy. It was about self-reliance, independence, individuality, having a go. That was the essence of *Sniffin' Glue.* The punk bands took up guitars and basses they could hardly play, while he wrote a fanzine in which the prose needed only to be understandable; nothing more fancy. No frills, no pretentions, no bull. It was a real communication from the kids of the street, kicking aside rubbish, spraying walls with graffiti, fuming at the way society dealt with them. It needed to be *heard.*

This was a change from passive consumption to active living. Watching Yes and Led Zeppelin had been fun and enjoyable for a while and there had been interaction between fans inside the venue, but the distance between fan and band, and the lack of opportunity for meaningful interaction meant concerts were in essence a passive experience. That meant they inculcated as much ennui as they did interest. Punk, on the other hand, was radically different. The audience experience, though at a much higher energy, was essentially the same – they saw a band on stage presenting their wares. But punk encouraged *fan* input, which for Perry was the fanzine, and which for many others was fashion, other fanzines, or forming a band. Innumerable bands were inspired by the early punk gigs. Nothing similar had happened after the last Zep tour, nor even when that group started out. The music biz then had existed in something of a rarified atmosphere, with infamous managers, ultra-rich musicians and a paucity of fan interaction. Punk developed like the electric telegraph: it was a communicative form enthusing everybody it touched, a street network, cast far and wide by photocopying, enthusiasm and persistence. This was the D.I.Y. ethic at work.

For all that he supported punk's aspirations to individualism, Perry was a bit of a purist, and by the time 1977 was underway he was beginning to fall by the wayside. The demise of *Sniffin' Glue* was nigh. He could see bands formerly declaring they would never sign a record deal signing record deals. Some even went on *Top Of The Pops*. The phrase *sell-out* began to spread, and the movement acquired a new set of wannabes and hangers on. Some of those characters went on to form terrific bands, while others kept the pure punk faith: no selling out, no compromise. But soon enough there came a fragmentation in the movement of the various breeds of purist. In an early issue of the 'zine, he and Joe Strummer of The Clash discussed the wearing of flared trousers by musicians. Strummer said no, Perry said, who cares? If people want to do their own thing, that's fine. *That's* punk. Strummer disagreed.

Perry was also feeling the urge to flex his own musical muscles. Alternative TV was his punk band, set up with friend Alex Fergusson, who by 1977 had enough contacts to begin work at Industrial Records studios, playing with the legendary Genesis P-orridge on drums. They had already released the song *Love Lies Limp* as a flexi-disc on the front cover of the final issue of the fanzine. Soon there were gigs too – they made their debut supporting another well regarded band of the time, The Adverts. The band lived on the edge of the punk movement, combining short thrash songs with lengthier experimental pieces, but they suffered from various line up changes and variations in direction. Soon, they found themselves separated from the scene, and even from a music press which had previously supported them.

Perry exhorted his readership to start their own punk projects, emphasising the D.I.Y. element and the ethic of standing apart from the mainstream. What he feared was a diminution of his independence, in the music he was making, the words he wrote, and in his lifestyle, through assimilation into the broader remit of music journalism. Decades later he published the complete set of back issues as *Sniffin' Glue: The Essential Punk Accessory*, giving a new generation of readers access to those heady days.

The fanzine in its earliest incarnation was an accidental template for the movement. Perry was skint and lacked proper equipment for his task, using an old children's typewriter on which to write. Felt pens made headlines and removed unwanted typos. While these in due course, and even at the time, became punk modes of operation, they owed their existence to Perry having no alternative. His energy, infectious amongst his peers, demanded that he use whatever was available. He was, after all, a man on a mission.

And even he, who feared being absorbed by the mainstream, took advantage of how keen the local record shops were to sell more of his 'zine. Those shops would advance him cash to write and create more issues, so in due course, when circulation figures really began to rise, the publication was assembled by printers. Yet that commitment to doing it yourself never faded; it just changed format and media.

Chapter 11

The Roxy

The Roxy Club in Covent Garden's Neal Street opened on Tuesday 14 December 1976 with the impressive opening line up of Generation X and Siouxsie and the Banshees. Don Letts was the DJ that evening, playing reggae from a cubicle filled with weed smoke. Despite early misgivings from some, over two hundred punters turned up to enjoy an amazing and, as it turned out, historic night. Bands playing later that week included The Heartbreakers, their audience filled with every punk luminary in the book. Generation X would return, and New Years Day saw the Roxy hosting Chelsea and The Clash. It was the beginning of something epic.

Andrew Czezowski and his partner Susan Carrington were at the heart of this punk explosion. As promoters of music at the Roxy Club, they worked with most of the important figures in punk, not least The Damned, whom Czezowski managed until August 1976. I asked him about his early experiences at the Roxy, especially what he felt about that force against the establishment which is usually cited as punk's origin. I wondered whether punk was more about something new and independently exciting, regardless of the existence of the establishment.

I am very concerned that when things are written in retrospect, there is too much research on other people's research, and newspaper articles or books written after the time, all feeding on each other and maintaining a narrative which may not have been true at the time. Malcolm McLaren was a great one for embellishing it all and appearing as someone with a vision, but he was a chancer. This one worked out for him. It was no more than a free-for-all fun time; yes, anarchic, but not in a conscious way, just youth full of anti-authoritarian anger and a need to express oneself in what was a changing social and political time of dramatic change, dragging the nation into a new progressive period. For some, it didn't work out so well, but change has casualties.

The band roster at the Roxy Club was impossible to beat. I asked Czezowski about punk beginning to get noticed in the second half of 1976. I wondered whether he felt he was at the heart of it all, and was even becoming the source of a lot of the punk band record contracts that were being signed at the time.

We didn't have time to think. It really took on a life of its own, and frankly we weren't too aware of what we effect we had as our lives spiralled around booking, buying beer, setting up the nights, sleeping and repeating.

I asked whether or not they were night owls.

We were night owls naturally, so the night life suited us and that rhythm became our norm. But we grow and adapt, and now we are larks.

Life as promoters of the Roxy was complicated, however.

Unfortunately, as the promoters, we didn't have the luxury of enjoying the bands – too many issues on the door, with tickets, the bar, beer, fights… you get the picture.

And there were periods of hand-to-mouth living.

We were at an age when our arrogance and ignorance were a protection. We had a great deal of self-belief, and felt "we can do this." Sure, there were loads of fuck-ups and we needed financial help. Dolly [Carrington's mother] was a saviour indeed, and a true Punk. She had the attitude: let's go for it.

Later, Czezowski and Carrington would put together the groundbreaking live LP *The Roxy Album, London WC2* which captured the atmosphere of the club and featured X-Ray Spex, The Adverts, Wire and Buzzcocks amongst others. But this release had a tortuous birth, and only appeared after great effort was expended. I asked Czezowski what he made of it now. Was it a kind of social commentary – a record of historical truth?

> *We recently had the quarter inch tapes baked to reseal them onto the plastic. During that time we copied them onto a PC to digitise the reels. We definitely feel this has stood up over time, and should be seen as a turning point in record companies' attitude to punk. It is a unique record of the times, and has never been repeated.*

Chapter 12

Stiff Records, Rough Trade, & More

Jake Riviera and David Robinson had been employed in Britain's burgeoning music scene for a while. Robinson had connections to the Jimi Hendrix Experience and later managed pub circuit veterans Brinsley Schwarz. Riviera managed another pub rock band, Dr Feelgood. The pair were energised by the punk explosion, starting Stiff Records to ride the wave. In classic British ironic style they took the label name from the phrase for a record industry failure: a stiff. (The label had started out as Demon Records.)

With songwriter and main man Nick Lowe at the centre of Brinsley Schwarz, it was an obvious step to have him record the debut Stiff 45. So it was that on 14 August 1976 a single entitled *So It Goes* was released by the label. The record sold well, but the Pink Fairies follow up did not go so well, albeit not quite a stiff. It was not long before they picked up a hot new band at the centre of the punk movement called The Damned, whose high octane classic *New Rose* would mark the official opening of punk on vinyl.

As 1976 turned into 1977, further acts jumped on board, including Elvis Costello, a.k.a. Declan MacManus, a musician who would go on to make sizeable waves in punk and the New Wave which followed. Also around were Ian Dury, soon to make it big, and Wreckless Eric, who, though a bit of a punk character, did not garner quite the same level of publicity and success as his peers.

Riviera and Robinson were determined to challenge the music biz orthodoxy of prog rock, glam, and the corporate framework which supported it: big offices, big wallets, gatefold sleeves and high art. Their philosophy was encapsulated in some of the slogans they spat out: *If It Ain't Stiff It Ain't Worth A Fuck* and *The World's Most Flexible Record Label.* Not only was their intention to record music quick and cheap, they wanted their records out fast. They wanted new bands and artists, nothing stale. They wanted to improvise, to duck and dive, to connect with the new street movement in London already calling itself punk. Though they dealt in vinyl and were no fly-by-night organisation, their attitude matched the punk D.I.Y. ethos. The major record labels had major bands. Stiff had street bands.

Declan MacManus meanwhile, having managed to get a demo tape into the hands of the Stiff supremos, became Elvis Costello and gave the label its first top 20 hit in 1977: *Watching The Detectives.* His *Top Of The Pops* appearance, so different to the usual cringeworthy performances, was impossible to forget once seen. It all added to the sense that something different was happening in music, that the old order was being challenged by upstarts. Riviera and Robinson knew that. Commercial success would bring new life to a tired old business.

It was perhaps The Damned who epitomised the part chaotic, part ordered attitude of the label and its founders. Their debut album on Stiff Records, *Damned Damned Damned,* was over in half an hour and consisted of a number of thrashing, razor-wit classics. The gunk-soaked cover was unforgettable, pushing Roger Dean and the rest far into the distance.

Geoff Travis was the man behind the first Rough Trade record shop, which he set up in West London in 1976. Until then the majority of vinyl had been sold through traditional shops such as HMV and Our Price. For this reason, the rules of interaction between fans and LPs were much the same as between musicians and record labels: them and us, big versus small, with the buyer having a choice of what the corporations deigned to offer.

When the Rough Trade shop opened, it was possible for a new band to press up their own single or EP and take it to Travis in Kensington Park Road. If he liked it, he would stock it. This simple route recommended itself to the upcoming punk bands of the capital city since it bypassed the obvious obstacles blocking their way – the monoliths of the music business, namely record companies and record store chains. Though some bands wanted to get signed, some others did not. The D.I.Y. ethic of the movement said they should get on and do it independently. Many did exactly that.

Soon, a new network of independent shops existed separately from the major chains, with word of mouth and street gossip the vital telegraph between bands and their fans. This was a network of committed, energetic enthusiasts, giving a two-fingered salute to what they saw as a Goliath-sized industry. Though nobody knew it at the time, Travis' vision, the indie shop network and the punk ethos all led to the end of the stranglehold music biz tradition had on the British market. It really was a revolution. Moreover, in due course it spread from London to other cities and towns across the nation.

Now, record shops were not just lines of LPs stacked in alphabetic order next to a handful of tills, they were more like operational headquarters for something vital, something brand new, something *exciting*. Punk was energy. It was *active*. It demanded that its acolytes live their own lives in their own way, celebrating their individuality and creative vision.

Being an active human being is not only important to life, it is psychologically necessary. That is the only way we grow. From 1976 onwards this applied to the essentials of young punk lives: to gigs, to clothes, to hair, and to the audio products – 45s and LPs.

At the beginning, Travis himself only had sketchy notions of how to operate. He learned his business chops and marketing smarts mostly by doing the job – as a D.I.Y.er, just like the bands he supported. His intuitive, quick-witted style however recommended itself both to the musicians who sought him out and to the rapidly evolving nature of the market. This was a sea change in British music, and Rough Trade's early success told them they were getting it right. But in addition, it was democratising a formerly hierarchical and distant business which thrived as much on exploitation as on musical discovery.

Rough Trade was not just independent in the true spirit of punk, it was *genuine*. It stood for creative honesty and a new identity.

Independent record labels and record shops were all very well, but another monolith stood in the way of punk bands and the success they craved. That obstacle was the BBC.

At the time, the BBC was just about the only source of radio in the country. Pirate radio stations had broken through with the pop music explosion of the sixties, and one new BBC radio station, Radio 1, had poached a few offshore DJs to make its new station hip and happening. Yet, barring short wave, there was almost nothing else. In television there was some diversity: in radio, as good as none. Yet Radio 1 would in due course provide a practical method for punk bands to get heard as the seventies limped into its second half. One man would lead the way. His name was John Peel.

His real name was John Ravenscroft, but to the many fans who listened to his show he was just Peel – the only DJ who played the kind of music they loved. John Peel's entry into radio was, as is often the case in creative circles, a mixture of networking and good luck. Working as a journalist in America in the early 1960s, he was present in the crowd when Lee Harvey Oswald was assassinated. He made a start in his career by associating his Liverpool roots with those of The Beatles, then surfing Beatlemania's wave in America. In this manner he acquired friends and kudos. Returning to Britain for the cultural transformation of the mid-1960s, the Summer of Love and a proliferation of pirate radio ships, he was present at the founding of the BBC's youth station Radio 1, which he proceeded to subvert in his unmistakably droll manner. Soon enough he was a fixture there, loved by all true music fans.

Until punk arrived, Peel had been a fan of psychedelia and prog rock, supporting Pink Floyd, Tangerine Dream (whose Edgar Froese he wrote to, extolling the virtues of the band's *Atem* album), and many other patchouli-scented outfits. He had a love for *underground* music, however, of any form, and when he began hearing tracks by punk pioneers in the latter half of 1976 he was enthralled.

To see the effect of punk on this titan of the airwaves, Peel's annual Festive 50 is the best place to look. Voted for by listeners, who sent in their three favourite tracks of the year, the Festive 50 was a top fifty favourite cuts, which in 1976 was dominated by songs such as Zep's *Stairway To Heaven*, *Layla* by Derek & The Dominos (that is, Eric Clapton), and Floyd's twenty-three minute epic *Echoes*. The 1977 list had an entirely different character, with a song by The Motors topping the chart and also cuts by Rezillos, The Clash and the Sex Pistols. Pink Floyd and Neil Young made the grade, but the change in tastes was evident. 1978's list however was dominated by punk bands: Sex Pistols, The Clash, Stiff Little Fingers, Magazine and Buzzcocks. David Bowie and Lynyrd Skynyrd made appearances, and *Layla* was still present, but the writing was on the wall for earlier classics. They mostly vanished.

It was the end of the road for the old order. Punk had smashed its way through their comfortable slippers and wads of cash, not to mention their extended guitar solos. Youth was speaking now.

Virgin Records' Head of A&R Simon Draper got to know Peel well.

> *Peel was a champion of what you might call "extreme" music. He was a gentle man, and really liked the early Virgin Records sounds. In those days he was the only media outlet for such music. He found himself at a loose end some evenings in the hours before he did his radio show, and a couple of times invited himself around to my place for dinner. I think he was in love with music. What he liked about punk was that it was new, raw and direct. He loved that aspect of it.*

Another John Peel innovation was to invite bands in to record sessions. These sessions would come to assume immense importance in the musical world, with a number of classic performances recorded in service of the John Peel Show. To record a Peel session became something of a badge of honour for bands, particularly those the great man championed.

The Damned recorded two sessions for him in their early days, one in late 1976 consisting of *Neat Neat Neat, New Rose, So Messed Up, I Fall* and *Stab Your Back.* The second session from spring of the following year featured *Stretcher Case, Sick Of Being Sick, Feel The Pain* and *Fan Club.* Buzzcocks were also a session favourite, with their 1977 tracks including their classic *What Do I Get.* Neither The Clash (who walked out after recording a few backing tracks) nor the Sex Pistols got to record a Peel Session.

John Peel was radio's most magnanimous gatekeeper for new music. He knew his power and influence, but chose a path of modesty and an intentional mockery of the usual DJ technique, such as when he "forgot" to play a record at the right speed. His enthusiasm for punk and what followed was infectious, and he was loved by fans and musicians alike. In part, this was for his independent stance and musical freedom – totally punk. He was *genuine,* a true music lover, for whom safety was to be abandoned when something new and interesting came along. For punks and punk bands, he was essential. He was, in effect, part of the movement.

I spoke with Jon Webster, former managing director of Virgin Records, who recalled how the arrival of punk changed the way singles and LPs were distributed.

Anyone could make a record, but then the problem was making it available. Stiff Records began a distribution deal with Rough Trade. The Rough Trade shop would take LPs on consignment – the lucky bands would get played on John Peel's show. I ran the Virgin shop in Birmingham during 1976, we would get stuff from smaller labels through our central warehouse, including from Stiff Records. I remember we had the Nick Lowe single in, 'So It Goes.' The boxes were taken into our shop, but if we sold out we had to wait up to a week to receive more. That was the "cottage industry" aspect – an alternative distribution system. It wasn't easy having to wait to get more copies of something popular. I remember punk customers were youthful and excited. But there was no general punk thing in those early days, they were more music fans. I was keen to sell them stuff, but I sensed something changing in the music business.

Jon also worked at the Manchester store.

The Virgin shop in Manchester sold punk records. We were ahead of the crowd in that regard, I think. We had stock by less well-known bands such as Eater. Our regular customers would come in to buy that kind of thing, and in time we became known locally for it. That turned into a bit of a problem, because the shop became a punk hang-out, even though it was small and there wasn't room for a crowd. We got too popular! Nobody else could get inside the shop sometimes. If the punks wouldn't leave, we had to get the police in to move them on. But having regular customers was good. I remember there was one guy who would come in, slap £15 on the counter, and ask for three of the latest imports. Those were exciting times for us and for them. We had a record deck to play music in the shop, the punks would want 'Pretty Vacant' on all the time. 'White Riot' was another outstanding single. Then the snowball effect started, and punk was everywhere. I remember the NME reviewing 'Marquee Moon,' we had twenty-five copies and they sold out in a day because of that write-up.

Jon's store was visited by some individuals who in later years would become iconic characters in British music.

> *People would come in to ask us for advice about getting a single out. I remember one time, this guy came in and handed over a cassette of his music. He said his band was called Warsaw. That turned out to be Ian Curtis.*

Chapter 13

100 Club Punk Special

The 100 Club in Oxford Street had been active for well over thirty years by the time punk hit it. Founded in 1942 at number 100, it had originally been the Feldman Swing Club, changing to the 100 Club half way through the 1960s. A home to jazz and, following the success of the Merseybeat sound, various British beat combos, in September 1976 it hosted a two-day punk event, one which would in due course be seen as a turning point for the movement.

The 100 Club Punk Special (latterly known as the 100 Club Punk Festival) was a two-day event organised by Ron Watts, who wanted to take advantage of the punk music beginning to bubble up from those London streets in which it had been fomented. Knowing Malcolm McLaren's influence on the scene, Watts approached him, suggesting that the Sex Pistols headline the event. Enthused by the response, both The Clash and The Damned, the latter about to release their groundbreaking *New Rose* single, signed up, with other bands either volunteering themselves or brought in by McLaren.

Music press support was critical to the event. By now, the *NME* and *Melody Maker* in particular had caught the punk vibe, and were enthusiastic in their support of bands and the scene as a whole. Caroline Coon of *Melody Maker* worked hard to make sure the event was publicised and attended as well as possible. Midway through September, eight bands were ready to play at the event, set for 20 and 21 September 1976.

The five lesser-known bands were: Siouxsie and the Banshees, Buzzcocks, Chris Spedding with The Vibrators, Subway Sect, and the French band Stinky Toys, persuaded to play by McLaren.

Siouxsie Sioux was a member of the Bromley Contingent, who in a few short weeks would make her television debut on the Bill Grundy Show, playing up to his faux-lecherous advances. Her look was unique, while her extraordinary vocals and music would soon define her as a major figure in the punk movement.

At the Pistols' Screen On The Green gig on 29 August, Siouxsie, Steve Severin and Billy Idol asked Malcolm McLaren if they could appear at the 100 Club Punk Special. He agreed to this request. Now the trio had to think of a name for the band. Severin, inspired by the horror film *Cry Of The Banshee,* got the last part, and Suzie – not then Siouxsie – got the first. Then Siouxsie had to come up with a band. The one she ended up with on the night was a four-piece: herself on vocals, Sid Vicious on drums, Steve Spunka – only later to become Steve Severin – on bass (which he was taught by Idol) and Marco Pirroni on the guitar. With Idol vanishing days before the gig to join Chelsea, on 20 September they performed as the quartet Suzie and the Banshees for the first time.

On 19 September the four assembled at a rehearsal room in Camden used by The Clash, where the basis of the performance was discussed. Legend has it that little actual music was played.

Their 100 Club set was recorded on one of the lo-fi cassette machines of the time, its microphone inbuilt, the sound quality pretty bad. Yet the atmosphere of the performance can easily be imagined from this sonic artifact. The drums took a medium tempo beat, without cymbals or fills (Vicious said he would play as part of the group only if he didn't have to touch the cymbals or sing). This gave the music a martial quality. The guitar thrummed, and occasionally rose solo over the sonic stew, but it was Siouxsie's voice which was the main attraction, even then, on her first public appearance as a singer and with no prior experience, sounding much as she would in later years: imperious and exotic. Her unique voice was recognisable at once, sometimes screaming or howling, usually chanting, sometimes a little softer, elsewhere dipping into silence as Pirroni wrestled a few half-strangled solos from his guitar. There was no tune as such, instead a stomp through improvised musical territory. Siouxsie incorporated elements of the Lord's Prayer into her lyrics, while Severin and Pirroni lifted a few of their riffs and licks from known songs, including the rock 'n' roll standard *Twist & Shout.*

There was plenty of cheering and whistling at the end, though the crowd would have heard nothing like it in their short lives. Many, however, had already decided to slope off, to quieter, less challenging locations. The band, at the end of their set, joined them.

Buzzcocks were one of Manchester's finest, formed by Pete Shelley and Howard Devoto, inspired by the energy and uncompromising attitude of the Sex Pistols. Chris Spedding was a well-known and experienced session guitarist who in the very early days of punk lent a hand in various capacities, including production duties. The previous year he had even managed a hit single, *Motor Bikin'*. The Vibrators meanwhile were a punk band formed that year, soon signed to the RAK record label. They knew Spedding, and had even been used as backing musicians for his song *Pogo Dancing*.

Subway Sect was led by the unique figure of Vic Godard, a singer-songwriter who became enamoured of punk almost as soon as it began to appear. After he and others began following the Sex Pistols, the dynamism and sheer energy of the movement inspired them to form their own band – one of punk's earliest. Subway Sect eventually found their way into the hands of Clash manager Bernie Rhodes, and soon they were gigging and recording music.

Stinky Toys were Parisian punks brought over by Malcolm McLaren. They had minor success, and after a couple of years split up.

Some elements of the festival were well-organised, others less so. The Sex Pistols, having gigged for a while, and with their own fans and local notoriety, found headlining the event well within their capabilities. The Damned and The Clash were also tight units with more than enough material to play. Chris Spedding and The Vibrators however were somewhat less prepared, The Vibrators not having been around as a unit for long. Legend has it that Spedding taught his new backing musicians various songs in the dressing room. There was no rehearsal. Siouxsie and the Banshees had similarly faced a dilemma, with the nascent quartet going on stage to perform what turned out to be an improvised performance. They had no intention of carrying on as a band afterwards – as Siouxsie said later, at the time that seemed absurd. Yet the following year all of this would be turned on its head.

Like the Sex Pistols' legendary gig at Manchester's Lesser Free Trade Hall on 4 June 1976, which various members of various famous bands were supposed to have attended (some did), the 100 Club Punk Special attracted characters soon to acquire their own fame and fortune. Verifiable attendees included Colin Newman of Wire, Shane MacGowan, in due course a Pogue, Paul Weller, whose band The Jam would strike out from punk roots in a most distinctive way, various other members of the Bromley Contingent, and Viv Albertine of The Slits, a band who would prove critical to the place of women in the punk movement. Various members of soon-to-be punk band The Adverts also attended, alongside Jah Wobble, a friend of John Lydon, who would after the demise of the Pistols form Public Image Limited with him.

Although three of the bands on the event's roster were well known and would go on to make weighty contributions to the British music scene, this comparatively small festival was a turning point for the cohesiveness of the movement, as fashions, music styles, individuals and managers all merged into a seamless whole. This was *punk,* 20/9/76, and it had arrived. And like that Manchester Pistols' gig organised by Shelley and Devoto, this couple of nights proved to be inspirational. There was no mistaking how much energy had been unleashed, how much anger expressed. It was visceral, exciting, transformational.

After year upon year of musical blandness, escapist glam and stadium rock conveyed by Kafka-esque organisations like the BBC, this street movement, with its call-to-arms of "Get off your arse!" "Do it now!" and "Do it yourself!" felt like the trumpets of the apocalypse blasting out of central London. The time was now, the D.I.Y. ethic undeniable, the energy infectious. It was speed and high-octane fuel rolled into one explosive pill. These bands, these individuals, these mesmeric characters like Lydon and Siouxsie, Dave Vanian and Joe Strummer, were the new role models. They had done it, so anyone could. That was the message – a message of hope for young people in a buttoned-up, beige country falling apart at the seams.

1976 was a cultural reset: a Year Zero. Like the 100 Club Punk Special itself, 1976 proved to be the beginning of a sea-change in British music. Post-1976 could only be different. The post-Punk Special music scene could only be different. There was no doubting that. Around six hundred people, queueing up and down Oxford Street in keen anticipation, now knew the truth. Some of them would go on to be the movers and shakers of that different future, with all the shocks, joys, tragedies and disasters

W.F.E. PROMOTIONS
PRESENTS AT
THE TIDDENFOOT
LEISURE CENTRE
LEIGHTON BUZZARD

SATURDAY 30TH OCTOBER
The DAMNED + CAUGHT IN THE ACT
Spearheading the Punk Rock Revival!

SATURDAY 13TH NOVEMBER
The Aylesbury ★ BUCKS
Kris Needs / Paul Kendall / Robin Bouit
Fraser Pearson / Colin Keinch

Printed advert for The Damned, collection of Kevin Shepherd. (*Used with permission*)

nted photo of The Damned, collection of Lynn Lee. (*Used with permission*)

Sex Pistols, Paradiso Amsterdam, 06-01-1977. (*Public domain*)

John Lydon, Paradiso Amsterdam, 06-01-1977. (*Public domain*)

Hand-made badge made by an employee of Virgin Records, collection of John Webster. (*Used with permission*)

he Maniacs & Dave Goodman, photo by Ian Dickson. (*Used with permission*)

Joe Strummer on stage.
(*Public domain*)

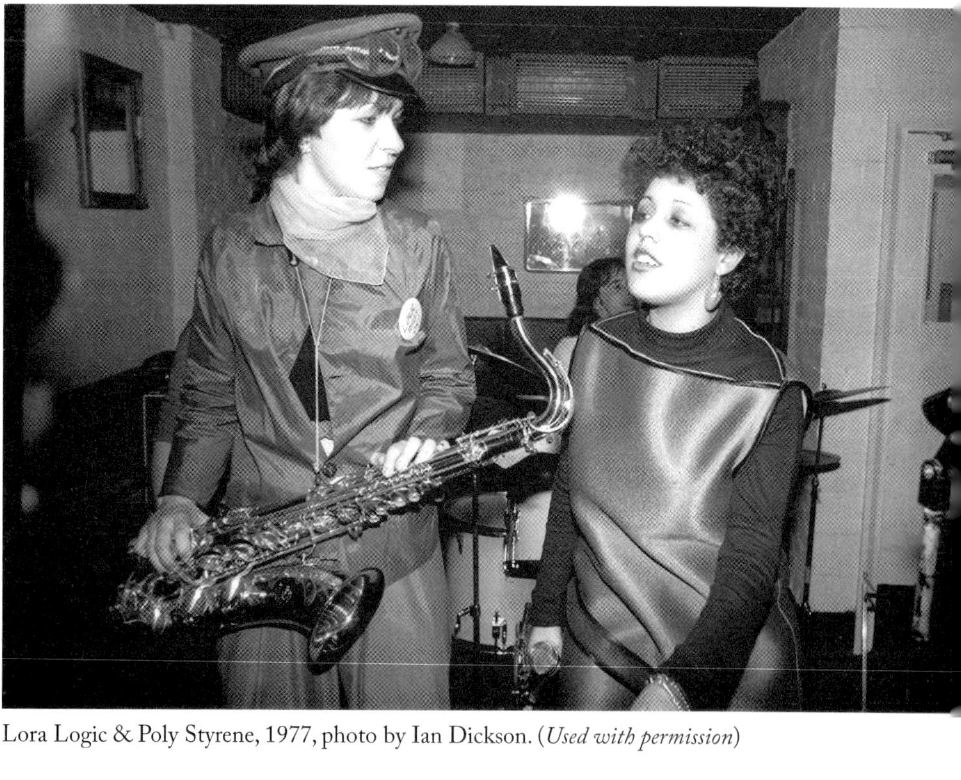

Lora Logic & Poly Styrene, 1977, photo by Ian Dickson. (*Used with permission*)

The Vibrators, 1977, collection of John "Eddie" Edwards. (*Used with permission*)

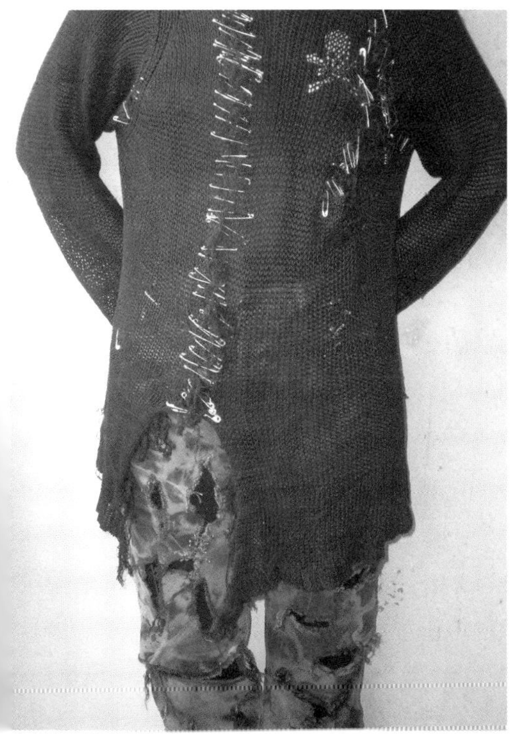

Punk fashion: safety pins used to hold clothes together. (*Public domain*)

John Peel. (*Public domain*)

Siouxsie Sioux on stage. (*Public domain*)

cond wave punk rockers, Zuiderpark, Den Haag, 05-07-1981. (*Public domain*)

nk mohican hair style. (*Public domain*)

Jean-Jacques Burnel, BSF Festival, 2012. (*Public domain*)

Punk's Not Dead graffito. (*Public domain*)

it promised. Some would simply stand and take it all in. Not one single person remained unmoved.

The charismatic individuals of the punk movement showed those in their audience that they did not ache alone. This was a revelation to many. Those old enough to be present at the Punk Special and just about of adult age had enough memories of the fluffy, colourful haze at the end of the 1960s to realise that when it departed, in ugliness, in brutality, through infighting, fracture and hedonistic narcissism, nothing took its place. In Britain, they saw the slightly twee, slightly childish glam scene, prog rock and chart pop music, none of which did much for working class youths living on council estates. None of these musical genres spoke of British boredom, English disillusionment, shite schools and shite jobs at the end of them. When John Lydon in particular appeared on stage at the Punk Special, his vocals, his diction, his manner and the rage in the so-called Lydon stare was a physical experience as well as an almost spiritual one. Likewise for the rest of the band, in musical format. Lydon embodied youthful feelings and showed how to express them: frustration, ennui, hopelessness, depression, isolation. He emerged like a snapping, gaudy monster from rubbish bins left to rot in the streets, to bite his fans and infect them with their own rage and passion.

Live music often does this – *feels* like this. Only occasionally does it overflow to become a cultural phenomenon.

Not all punks were enamoured of the nihilistic side of the movement – the anarchy, the chaos, the destructiveness. One incident at the 100 Club Punk Special, although most likely one with unforeseen consequences for its drunk, drugged-up instigator, has come to epitomise the violence that walked hand in hand with a lot of punk gigs.

The Damned were playing on the second day of the event. Members of the audience noted that Dave Vanian had become agitated about a smashed glass, thrown by a punter and fragmenting on a supporting pillar. Word soon got around that a member of the audience had been seriously injured by a shard entering her eye. Later accounts identified Sid Vicious as the cause of the incident. Whether or not he intended to bring chaos and cause bodily harm is a moot point, though the beer glass was aimed at Vanian himself. But the consequence was that the young woman who was the victim was blinded in her injured eye. Vicious was arrested and spent a few days in prison, visited by some of the punk luminaries of the time, including Viv Albertine and Vivienne Westwood.

Sid Vicious would do things at gigs none of the Pistols would consider, though, once his self-destructive streak was observed and comprehended, his tendency to speed-fuelled violence began to be exploited, not least by that arch-manipulator Malcolm McLaren, for whom all publicity was good publicity. Vicious, obsessed with the Sex Pistols and learning bass guitar by copying The Ramones, was cannon fodder for some of the dark angels surrounding punk's iconic band. He could be relied upon to be a danger. That an innocent audience member lost her sight in one eye was a consequence of this reliance on nihilism and shock.

I wondered what Andrew Czezowski's abiding memories were of the 100 Club Punk Special.

We had feeling of raw energy in the crowd and on stage, chaotic and passionate. We arrived late on Watts' [100 Club booker Ron Watts] guest list. As we were on the stairs, the medics were coming out with the girl who had splintered glass that cut her eye.

Virgin Records A&R head Simon Draper was another attendee of the 100 Club Punk Special.

I did find punk music a bit too aggressive. When the Sex Pistols played, I could feel that aggression in the audience. Yet it was exciting too. We had a bit of an office argument after the gig, some of us were enthusiastic, some of us not…

Overall, the vibe of punk's two-day festival was inspirational, but the movement was far more than an artistic and social breakout. Anger is an *energy*, as has been noted. It is unpredictable, and like all emotions is difficult to control. In fact, human evolution has ensured that it should not be controlled, since its content must be heard. Like joy, like fear, like embarrassment, anger is a message from deep inside the human subconscious, bringing word of frustration. Such messages, if repressed in a society like Britain's, are liable to burst out without warning. Punk was a medium of frustration, spiralling out of control in some quarters, elsewhere more philosophical, sometimes the instigator of broader social trends. It was a multi-headed beast from forgotten council estates, part music, part fashion, part ethic. But it had an underbelly which made it vulnerable.

Chapter 14

The Anarchy Tour

Scheduled for early December 1976, the Anarchy In The U.K. Tour was intended to showcase the best punk had to offer, including the Sex Pistols, The Damned, The Clash, and America's Johnny Thunder & The Heartbreakers. These punk notables had their own tour bus and much else to recommend their new lifestyle, but there was a problem. A couple of days earlier Bill Grundy had presided over a television swear-fest of catastrophic proportions, giving the Pistols the publicity they needed, but making them too hot to handle. Already, the lily-livered locals of various English shires were finding themselves frightened of those two little words: Sex Pistols. In the newspapers all talk was of the filth and the fury. Black-and-white photographs of punks in their "outlandish" clothes covered the front pages. This was problematic.

The first date (quaintly titled "A Punk Rock Evening") was in Norwich at the University of East Anglia, but the chancellor of that institution had the gig cancelled on the grounds of public safety and the protection of his bricks and mortar. A student sit-in protest resulted. The tour was therefore postponed until 6 December, when the bands were due to show up at Leeds Polytechnic. Chaotic days saw other cancellations and new arrangements, with dates at the Electric Circus in Manchester, in Caerphilly, in Cleethorpes, and at the Woods Centre in Plymouth.

Boredom by Buzzcocks could have been the tour's lead song. With too much time spent boozing in hotel rooms, nobody had much of a sense of what was happening outside the goldfish bowl they were trapped in. The frustrated musicians spent as many hours reading about themselves in the national papers as they did sound-checking and playing. Television was their only other comfort, and that was not saying much.

Freelance writer Steve Hardy recalled those crazy days.

A relative of mine was on the committee that got the Derby King's Hall gig banned…I kept a very low profile about that for YEARS afterwards! I believe the committee were okay with the other bands on the bill playing as advertised, but requested that the Sex Pistols play a sort of matinee show for them first. Not surprisingly, Malcom McLaren refused, and so the gig was pulled. Quite how much say the other bands had in that decision is open to question, though I understand The Damned were booked into different hotels from the others, so they were probably even more removed from the decision-making process than the Heartbreakers and the Clash.

The Derby gig was meant to happen on 4 December. John Peel intended seeing the Sex Pistols that night, but it did not happen – indeed, he never saw the group play live during their ascendancy. He had attended a 100 Club gig on 11 May that year, when the band were enjoying a Thursday night residency, but left during the opening song to go and present his radio show. He did drive up to Derby on the 4th to see the band, but when he arrived all he found was a hand-written note attached to the door declaring that the gig had been cancelled.

However, not everyone who saw the Pistols or other punk bands was able to appreciate music's brave new direction. Rainbow Theatre front-of-house man Hal Harries recalled:

I remember seeing the Sex Pistols at Walthamstow Town Hall, although I think it was by accident – I wanted to see Hatfield & The North. The Sex Pistols were one of the support bands. There were not many people there, and to be honest nobody paid them much attention. It was a bit of a cacophonous noise! I didn't think it was terribly musical. But punk was so much more raw. Too raw, perhaps. I didn't feel the punk musicians could play well enough. But I did like The Clash, they were a bit more musical, less primitive. I liked The Stranglers too. They were much more musical, and therefore more attractive to me. The atmosphere at the Rainbow Theatre when they played in January 1977 was exciting, with a bit of an "anti-establishment" vibe. That was the gig when Hugh Cornwell's "Fuck" T shirt got the band's set curtailed.

But Lydon himself was not quite the man he presented himself onstage:

Johnny Rotten used to come along to Rainbow gigs, I think he lived just up the road. He got a lot of negative press, but in person he was a nice bloke, I liked him. He usually came in on his own, not with a crowd, and he was friendly. I remember when Bob Marley & The Wailers played in June 1977, we shared a joint at the back of the venue.

Virgin Records MD Jon Webster also recalled a memorable meeting with the man:

Some time after punk, when Lydon was doing Public Image Ltd, I had lunch with him and a colleague of mine. He was genial. He seemed to lack boundaries, as if he was fearless. I remember we went to a Japanese restaurant. He took a lump of wasabi and snorted it up both nostrils. "Ah, that's the way to clean out the sinuses!" He was very good company.

Simon Draper, Virgin Records' A&R head, also got to know Lydon quite well.

As the singer of the band, he had to fight off Malcolm McLaren all the time. McLaren didn't want people to think Lydon had any musical credibility, but I found out that Lydon liked Van Der Graaf Generator, amongst other groups, which surprised me. When Lydon did a solo Capital Radio interview and this fact came out, McLaren was furious. Lydon liked Can too. He was friendly in person, but he could be rude. I thought he was highly intelligent – and good fun. His stage persona was a different part of him, aggressive and sarcastic. His looks, that pale skin and ginger hair, gave him stage charisma. But off stage he was different. I remember one time we went for a Japanese meal, and he paid using his American Express Gold card, which seemed rather incongruous to me! He was into reggae also, and liked to listen to it on my Buckingham loudspeakers. In the end he bought them off me and took them to his house in L.A.

With all the tour chaos, inter-band relationships began to get fractious. In just days The Damned were off the tour. According to Brian James, this was because of Malcolm McLaren's increasingly manipulative attitude to promotion. The Pistols had hardly ever played outside of London, whereas trailblazers The Damned were veterans in comparison. McLaren had therefore wanted The Damned as part of the Anarchy tour to broaden audience appeal. But in the aftermath of the Derby gig decision, with The Clash and Johnny Thunder unwilling to let the Sex Pistols down, solidarity was key, and The Damned's motives looked to some like disloyalty to the tour. Arguments, tension and broken promises resulted.

There was also the issue of the Bill Grundy incident. It was for the Anarchy tour that the Pistols had been rehearsing when they were forced by McLaren to appear on the show, thus releasing that notorious F-bomb. With The Damned not travelling with the other bands in the luxury tour bus – they were enjoying a grotty old Ford Transit van – other emotions began to get in the way of harmonious touring. Relations between McLaren and The Damned's management became strained. Again, according to James, this time corroborated by Captain Sensible, it was McLaren who demanded that The Damned slip down the performance roster, something James would not countenance.

In later years this story of The Damned being discarded would acquire a haze of misinformation, with everybody following a different version of the tale. Regardless of those stories, The Damned were cast aside, the tour became a disaster zone, and nobody enjoyed that, including the managers, the music paper photographers and the roadies. Only the national press, following the tour like vultures following a dying gnu, had the principles and ethical standards required to vicariously enjoy the omnishambles they were reporting on.

Chapter 15

Women In Punk – Siouxsie Sioux

In the mid-1970s, feminism was still a peculiar thing to the average male, an unexpected, perplexing, rather difficult phenomenon, at which they frowned, shaking their heads. From whence came all these sloganeering women? What did they want? And were they serious, or was it just some kind of fad that could safely be ignored once it was out of the newspapers and off the television screen?

The second wave of feminism which had its most visible manifestation in the 1970s was a consequence of the liberalism of the sixties. Basic rights had been fought for and, eventually, obtained by the feminist pioneers of the late 19th and early 20th centuries, with equality and problems of gender discrimination in the sights of the second wave. That discrimination, exploitation and abuse, rampant in British society as in most of the rest of the world, had a particularly stark manifestation in the music business. It is a mark of how entrenched male attitudes were back then that in 2024 it was still deemed necessary for newspapers to present shocking, tell-all reports on women's woeful positions and treatment in the music biz. Back in the seventies, it was just as bad, or worse.

There were plenty of women artistes around, but the overwhelming majority were solo performers, controlled by producers, record moguls, multinational corporations and the like, their image – their faces and their bodies, in essence – sold for male consumers and female wannabes. But mostly the scene was about young men, serious male artists, and reliable older men, such as those who had achieved fame during the war. Bands, moreover, were almost exclusively male. The number of all-women bands in the sixties and seventies can be listed on a single sheet of A4 paper: they include The Pleasure Seekers (featuring Suzi Quatro, soon to be a leather-clad solo artist), and Fanny, something of a pioneer group in a masculine world. The Runaways meanwhile were also pioneers.

As for the hardware side of things, that was as good as exclusively male. Engineers, studio technicians, producers, arrangers and conductors were male. The corporate money-jugglers were male. The corporations were male. The instrument makers and sellers were male. And the vast majority of the people in bands who played those guitars, basses, drums and keyboards were male. It was a time of unthinking, automatic entitlement, a simple truth of society: the way of the world. This, after all, was the *public* world, the theatre of events and progress, of action and development, where men played their role. It was *their* stage. Women's stage was the domestic sphere, where they were limited to a small number of roles, including domestic, mother, and support worker – all unpaid, of course. Handily for the men, they were expected to be the directors of the domestic sphere also, the head of the household, so even there they were in charge.

Alas for such men, it was necessary to let some women outdoors for the sake of a quiet life. There they were allowed to be sexual beings, almost always young, showing off their marvellous physiques and enchanting faces. But then... then something changed. It was 1976: a year of bad omen for masculine dominance.

Off the scene, decisions as yet unknown were being made which would play out with dramatic consequences. For instance, 1976 was the year that EMI signed one Catherine Bush, soon to become one of the greatest musicians of her era. Remarkably, the executives at that record label realised Bush, then eighteen, was too young to be introduced to the world, so they let her develop in peace for a couple of years. But above all, 1976 was the year of punk's fiery explosion, and being a D.I.Y. ethos that meant women should also do it themselves. And so they did.

One of the most striking, most remarkable and most driven of those women was Siouxsie Sioux, named Susan Ballion when she was born. Her father was an alcoholic scientist who had moved his family from Belgium to Britain, settling in Chislehurst, Kent. A home life of insecurity, distrust and isolation led Susan to become a child for whom imagination was a way out of illness and unhappiness, and who, in order to survive psychologically, had to develop an array of mental defences against the problems which beset her. When she reached her teens she saw that not only did she not fit into traditional British suburban society, her whole family did not. Childhood trauma and other social issues turned Susan – just nineteen when punk hit the headlines in that momentous year of '76 – into a woman protected by a suit of psychological armour, which allowed her some relief from the complexities, the contradictions and the cruelty of the world. Inside that suit, she could be safe. But armour, like the complex masks assumed by stage actors, often reflects the truth of inner character. Susan Ballion, for all that her father was bedevilled by addiction and unemployment, remained somebody who felt sympathy. He was a reader of books: a thinker. Likewise, herself. The young Susan Ballion was sensitive and highly intelligent, a facet of her persona yet to be noticed and acknowledged by the world. But that acknowledgment and its corresponding acclaim would not be long in arriving, though they would be offered to a woman quite unlike Susan Ballion. They were offered to a new character, an invented woman, with her own stance, look, style and message: Siouxsie Sioux.

The look was striking, startling, original. Moreover, it was displayed by a *woman*. Such a thing had rarely been seen before.

Early photographs show her with cropped hair, itself a singular gesture in a world where to be a sexual creature women had to have long hair, or at very least shoulder length. Short dyed hair was *different*. Indeed, much of the punk tradition of having short hair was a reaction to the standard long hair of earlier in the 1970s. But she was following the credo of the punk movement, which in that early epoch was all about individualism. Her eye make-up could be star-shaped, more often the "cat-eye" extended make-up which came to characterise her. Her jewellery, ear-rings for instance, had a tribal appearance. She wore a lot of black: black coat, black top, black boots. When her hair grew a little longer it was dyed black. She was a punk alright, but also a proto-goth.

Her eyebrows alone could be striking: square-edged, almost unfeminine. Yet she retained (and sometimes exploited) her sexuality as she devised new look after new look. She was a pioneer, simultaneously discovering herself and passing on the results of that journey to any who would take notice.

She came to public notice on 1 December 1976. Lurking in the background as Lydon & Jones mocked Bill Grundy on his infamous television show was a distinctive young woman with very short, bleached blond hair, one eye surrounded by a star of make-up, wearing a white top, black trousers held up by braces, and a spotted necktie. Unique, matchless, and bouncing around in mockery of Thames Television's twee music, she both railed against and sarcastically sucked up to Bill Grundy as he pretended to get it on with her. Her performance was brilliant: a true work of performance art. Even Lydon had to work hard to match her. While she gurned and danced as the credits rolled, braces akimbo and a fag in her hand, and as Grundy muttered "Oh shit" to himself, Lydon glanced down at his not-terribly-punk wristwatch to check what time it was.

The papers next day were full of the filth and the fury, but Siouxsie had also been spotted by eagle-eyed hacks: *Siouxsie's a Punk Shocker* was their headline, alongside a picture of her with downcast mouth. But she was unrepentant, explaining that the Sex Pistols and their language were important because they were the first band in her times to say or do anything worthwhile. Which, on that day, they were.

Soon Siouxsie and the Banshees were a band, their name a fixture, their front woman in the words of Viv Albertine of The Slits the only important thing at the 100 Club Punk Special. In one sense she was correct to say that, since bands of any sort were always blokes. A *girl* fronting a band, let alone a girl *band*, was shocking, unnatural, wrong. Girls could not play bass or drums, let alone that chosen instrument of musos, the electric guitar. Siouxsie, with her dangerous look and in-yer-face attitude – her refusal to follow feminine norms – was a trailblazer to many young women witnessing the punk explosion. She, Albertine, and indeed Kate Bush were breaking new ground. That to men it was hallowed ground made their rebellion all the more shocking.

Siouxsie and Steven Severin had intended breaking up their musical alliance after the 100 Club Punk Special, but they were asked to play a second time, so they found a new drummer to replace Sid Vicious, Kenny Morris, and placed Peter Fenton on guitar duties, though after a few months Fenton's rock leanings became too obvious and he was replaced. John McKay, however, was much more a Banshee, his gritty, glittering style eminently suited to the proto-goth songs the band were working on. Thus the early Banshees sound developed, fronted by Siouxsie's remarkable voice and McKay's clashing guitar textures, with Severin and Morris providing an earthy backdrop. Now a gigging entity, and with television exposure on Tony Wilson's *So It Goes* show, the band soon achieved that essential status of being John Peel sessioneers, recording a stunning, mesmerising set. The sound was cold yet with a beating heart, iced over with McKay's guitar patterns and grounded in a krautrock style drum beat – an almost industrial music, albeit made with chrome and neon, not steel and oil. Nobody, Peel not least, had heard anything like it.

Andrew Czezowski recalled her from his days at the Roxy Club – the opening night featured Siouxsie and the Banshees. I asked him what he recalled of her, of her stage presence and of her character as a young woman.

> *Siouxsie was a natural. You just had to watch her, she was much better than when we saw her at the 100 Club, and was a perfect support act for Generation X. Everything we did at the time was new and experimental; none of us really knew what we were doing. But what was more important was that we wanted to do it. Failure was not important. We were supportive of each other, as outsiders often are.*

So Siouxsie Sioux progressed, departing punk a year or so after it appeared, refining her sound, leading the way for countless other women who aspired to her look, freedom of expression and independence. She was a queen whose realm was the darkness at the back of each of her fans' minds. When punk passed away and the gothic landscapes of post-punk appeared, she was there to mark the way, her darkness acting as a nocturnal beacon, her brightness vivid in red lipstick.

Chapter 16

X-Ray Spex, Lora Logic, & The Slits

Poly Styrene was not her real name, yet it fitted the plastic accessories and dayglo hues of punk. Captain Sensible wore white plastic sunglasses, Poly Styrene kept her teeth braces. None of that disregard for cultural norms mattered to her. There was a free-for-all in fashion now, spearheaded by punk, yet already fragmenting into innumerable related styles; and she wanted to be part of that.

She was born Marianne Joan Elliott-Said, of mixed Scottish and Somali parentage and brought up in Brixton. During her teenage years she left home and travelled from free festival to free festival, an itinerant and sometimes perilous lifestyle, which in due course led her to the Pier Pavilion in Hastings. There, on 3 July 1976, she saw the Sex Pistols playing a gig. As with so many others of the time, she was inspired, and without delay began setting up a punk band, which she would call X-Ray Spex.

Her name accorded with the plastic mantle of one wing of the punk movement; its revelling in anti-fashion, its drive to individuality. Aware of her own complete lack of interest in fitting in with conventional British society, she revelled in the new freedom. She took her name from a non-fashion item: polystyrene.

Above all she rebelled against the standard young woman's identity of the time, that of sex object. Her path was that of an *individual,* which meant she could take any identity she wished. She assembled her stage name, her wardrobe, her hair style and those instantly recognisable dental braces in order to be herself rather than what society expected her to be – at the time, a rare act for a young woman. Like Siouxsie Sioux, she simply followed her own path regardless of the noise around her. She had not intended becoming a trailblazer, she was one by virtue of wanting to know where her personal trail went. She was a traveller and a cultural traveller, her clothes, hair and look all manifestations of her journey.

The band soon cohered. Jack Stafford played guitar, Paul Hurding sat behind the drum kit and Paul Dean played bass. The fifth member was Lora Logic, a schoolgirl saxophonist whose playing on the early singles gave X-Ray Spex a distinctive sound, further helping them to stand out in the new proliferation of punk bands.

X-Ray Spex produced a clutch of Top 40 singles and one of the most highly praised punk albums of the time, *Germfree Adolescents.* Even John Lydon, not known for an abundance of compliments, remarked that the band were great and unlike any other punk outfit. Poly's voice was another feature of the music critical to the band's success and high standing. Though she had attempted a commercially released reggae single (which bombed) when she was younger, she now sang in a much more liberated, lacerating, sometimes atonal style, her trademark squeal at the end of lyrics marking her out. She simply did it her own way, and if people liked that – great! With melodic songs and this captivating sound, the band was set for major success.

Poly was aware of her place as a striking front woman. The band's classic 1977 song *Oh Bondage Up Yours!* began with this paeon to women's place in society: *Some people think little girls should be seen and not heard, but I think… oh bondage, up yours!* Alas, it was not a hit – banned in their wisdom by the Beeb. Although the song was a diatribe against capitalist waste and artificiality, it also touched the feminist attitudes of the time. There was almost nothing like it around, certainly not in the commercially critical singles charts. And Poly actively stood against the prevailing male idea of the young woman as sex symbol, remarking that if anybody tried to make her one, she would remove that essential manifestation of female sexuality, her hair. When success began to take hold, she followed through with that deed.

She was not only a trailblazer, she was a *memorable* trailblazer. Like Siouxsie Sioux, once seen and once heard, she was unforgettable. To young women of the time she acted as a catalyst and a guide, granting their wishes, giving them permission to be themselves and stick two fingers up at male norms.

I spoke with Lora Logic about those early days with the band. How did she join?

I joined X-Ray Spex in autumn 1976. The initial advert in the music paper, which I answered, said: 'Young punks wanted.' That was the first time I heard the word, but I had no idea what it meant. Because it was totally different I was attracted to the advert – it had a good rebellious feel about it. I rang up, but the manager said they weren't really looking for another girl and they weren't really looking for a saxophone – they wanted traditional rock instruments. But he said come along anyway, because I was very enthusiastic.

I wondered how the early rehearsals went.

The second time I heard the word punk was at the first X-Ray Spex rehearsal. Poly and Falcon the manager were talking about these places where punk bands went to play, and where we were going to play, one of those being the Roxy – Falcon knew Andy Czezowski. With Poly being very much into clothes, designing her own clothes, and having a market stall on the King's Road with her friend Sophie – who sewed up Poly's ideas for clothes – there was talk about the way punks looked and dressed. This was before I actually saw punks. There was talk of safety pins and how the boys in X-Ray Spex should look: what was punky and what wasn't. So that was how I first became aware of the concept of punk.

Falcon, being an entrepreneur, was ambitious. He wanted to be like Malcolm McLaren. He wanted the X-Ray Spex sound to be raw and punky, and he talked about punk music having three chords and being very wild. We didn't really pay too much attention to that. We just got on with our music – it happened spontaneously. We formed our own sound around Poly's voice and lyrics. We were young and full of beans, so it was naturally punky.

Punk's cultural hub was the King's Road.

Poly and Falcon's house was quite near the King's Road, with all these alternative fashion market stalls. The King's Road was a very happening place, with lots of visitors. As soon as you went on it you noticed something new and different was in the air. That was punk. There was a certain uniformity; there were groups of people with safety pins and brightly coloured haircuts. That stemmed from Vivienne Westwood and Malcolm McLaren's shop SEX. I remember walking past that shop and seeing Jordan. That was kinda scary, because it was the very early days and she looked quite scary on the entrance of the shop – striking a pose. Who knew what was in there…

More and more I noticed this alternative energy. Punks were always buzzing, and jumping up and down when they walked – ripped up T shirts and lots of make-up. A lot of black clothes.

The Roxy Club became the home of those early punk rock bands. It was high-energy music, and it hit home that there were other bands like X-Ray Spex who had the same energy levels. Poly was already aware of what else was going on in the punk scene, but I wasn't so much aware of it all until that first gig at the Roxy.

I asked about Poly in those early days.

I'd been practicing the saxophone alone in my bedroom for quite a long time – at least a year or so. If I travelled anywhere with my family I would always take it with me, to practise. I was quite addicted. A time came when I really wanted to play with other people and join a band. Looking around me, there were only pub rock bands around the area I lived. There were a few music magazines, so I looked in the back of 'Melody Maker' and saw that advert. Something inside me propelled me to get on the train and go. It wasn't really an audition, because when I got to Falcon's house I was greeted by a giggling Poly Styrene, and the most amazing thing was we were wearing almost identical clothes. This was uncommon at that time – 1950s secretarial suits, matching jackets with pencil skirts, worn with low stiletto heels. So, that was bizarre! We'd got them from market stalls or somewhere like that. When I saw her at the front door, I felt as if I'd always known her.

This meeting had significant consequences for X-Ray Spex.

Falcon thought it would be an interesting prospect to have two young girls in the same band. He was sold on the idea of having a female saxophonist in the band. He was thinking quite ruthlessly in commercial terms. Poly thought it would be a fun idea. We got on very well, we laughed a lot. So they told me I was in the band from that first meeting. The second meeting was a rehearsal. We brainstormed the name of the band: X-Ray Spex. Poly and I sat in the kitchen and thought up that name.

Those early impressions of Poly (before I got kicked out) were that we were besties, and had a lot of giggles together. She was very extrovert and had strong creative ideas. I thought she was very talented, she had an amazing voice, and visionary lyrics. Her dress expressed her ideas through clothes and design. I loved working with her and being around her. We shared a lot in common, the musical chemistry was great. She really liked the saxophone. They soon saw that the raw sound of the sax could be extremely punky, and expressive. She was a very strong, charismatic personality.

She also had a secretive side, she was very insecure, like a lot of performers. On the one hand she appeared very extrovert, but another side of her was quite insecure. She revealed to me in those early days quite a few experiences from her childhood; very disturbing, dysfunctional experiences. Later on, in the years when we lived together in the Krishna Temple, looking back at all those things that she'd revealed to me, I understood why her bipolar kicked in so severely. Because of that, X-Ray Spex had to disband quite prematurely.

What about the early X-Ray Spex gigs?

All of the early gigs were incredibly special. Gigging was surreal and exciting, and spontaneous too. We weren't exactly over-rehearsed! Certainly at the Roxy, most bands celebrated if they got from the beginning of a song to its end in some kind of coherent way. We were probably more coherent than many other bands. The gigs were also memorable because the audience would often get on stage. Poly didn't really mind that, as long as they weren't on stage for the whole set. The energy was just out of this world. No-one knew what to expect, we didn't really know musically what was going to happen next. Sometimes it got a little bit scary, there were some extreme characters in the audience that took the punk spirit to an extreme. The drugs were quite extreme as well – a lot of amphetamines. Inebriation in the audience in very small clubs – that could get quite hairy, with a lot of shooting up too in the toilets. I didn't feel I wanted to hang around after I'd played…

One time my parents came to watch us, they dressed quite smart, they had no idea what punk was. They liked Poly, they thought she was quite charming! I did escort them out of the club as soon as possible...

The chemistry of X-Ray Spex was raw and unique. Poly sang the words to her songs with such determination and conviction, and of course her lyrics were quite ahead of their time. A lot of the punk bands didn't really have that much to sing about apart from destruction, but Poly was far more imaginative.

Lora Logic also followed a musical path which allowed her to be herself. Born Susan Whitby, she played on the earliest X-Ray Spex material. A highly talented saxophonist, her instrumental arrangements were used on the band's only album even though she had by then departed. She went on to form Essential Logic, then played in various bands. Her saxophone part on *Hey! Rise Of The Robots* by The Stranglers gave that song a sheen reminiscent of her work alongside Poly Styrene, one converting the hectic, clattering track into a futuristic adrenalin rush.

I asked her about her path in music.

I lived near Wembley Stadium, so the sort of music that was on my doorstep was mega-concerts like Fleetwood Mac, the Osmond Brothers and David Bowie. Bowie changed my whole world. I think if I'd lived in central London I would have picked up more of the punk changes.

Was the saxophone her first choice of instrument?

My Mum and Dad never had the opportunity to play musical instruments when they were growing up, or of developing any artistic skills. When my Mum came to England from Finland, and got married and had me, she was very keen that I get the opportunity to learn musical instruments. We went through a selection of instruments – violin, piano... At school, I liked the idea of playing music, but it was all terribly boring – practising on your own. I found it very tedious. I went through guitar, violin, piano... giving them all up quite quickly. I'd heard the saxophone a lot in rock 'n' roll, which I liked – Bill Haley and the Comets, and all those great 1950s saxophone riffs. But I never thought that Mum and Dad would buy me a saxophone.

Lo and behold, one day they did; a beautiful tenor saxophone. When I saw it, I have to admit that it was love at first sight. I took to the saxophone like a fish to water. I practised and practised – I used to play four or five hours a day, playing along to my favourite records, which largely consisted of David Bowie and T-Rex. And I used to like musicals, such as South Pacific and Godspell. My brother had those albums at home. I played along to those records in a clothes cupboard, to silence the very loud blast of my early saxophone squeaks. I took to it very naturally.

There was always jazz in the house – John Coltrane, Ornette Coleman, great saxophone players. I wasn't much of a fan, but my father, who was not well, was soothed by the music. I think that music went into my ears even though my mind told me I didn't like jazz. I was more into rock.

Neither her chosen instrument nor her appearance conformed to traditional female norms. With her curly hair cut short, on stage she would wear a macintosh coat and either a cap, a hat, or some other head covering. Short hair for women punks gave them a licence to reject the sex object trope and become something deeper, more authentic. These female punks were not quite a sisterhood, but the vibe was there.

Was there a strong feminist feeling in those days?

To be honest, I never really thought about it at the time, and I don't think Poly did either. They were labels that were put on her after punk – that with a song like 'Oh Bondage!' Poly was fighting for women's freedom. But she said herself that wasn't the idea behind the song at all, the idea was to fight against all forms of bondage – from a spiritual perspective, as she later commented. The ultimate bondage was being tied to the material world.

Certainly, when I started, we weren't thinking that we were men or women, it was an overall sense of freedom, of just coming from all corners and not having to be particularly technically proficient – just to be able to pick up an instrument and learn it as you went along, and be able to express yourself in any and every way that you wanted to. It was about complete creative freedom. I never thought about, oh, I'm in a girl's body and I'm doing this! I think all these male/female labels are much more prevalent now or in recent times than they ever were then. We were just teenagers, growing up, and we were enjoying the creative freedom that was offered to us. We were given places to play, and independent record labels, which popped up very quickly, giving us platforms to release our music, even if it wasn't very polished.

All these creative and technical breakthroughs like home recording made making music far more accessible; they smashed the old boys' network. That was more of an issue, smashing down those barriers. I didn't think Siouxsie, for instance, was fighting as a female warrior. It was more about being an individual.

But punk did help women.

Punk took away the stereotype of girls or women in the music business, because it was very much a business when punk broke through. It freed women up to be themselves, and not to worry about what they looked like, and not to feel obliged to look like a Barbie doll in public. That was freeing.

Girls felt they were accepted on their own terms by record companies, who were not so concerned with women looking like sex-bombs, because other visuals were there – a great variety. That was a good thing.

The Slits were also one of the more important manifestations of the punk movement. Formed in 1976, the first line-up included Suzy Gutsy and Kate Korus, with Palmolive (Paloma Romero) and Ari Up (Ariane Forster) also in the early band. Tessa Pollitt and Viv Albertine, the latter destined to become a punk legend, joined a little later. Albertine had been a member of The Flowers Of Romance, a non-playing, non-recording unit which featured a number of punk luminaries, including Sid Vicious and Keith Levene. Ari Up, upon meeting Korus and Palmolive, formed the band, and in due course they were supporting their friends The Clash on that band's White Riot Tour.

The early sound was rough and ready, but their style and sheer energy, and the fact that all members of the band were women, made them stand out. Their live shows emphasised the power of drumming, with Ari Up making as much as she could of her frontwoman position.

Lora Logic recalled an incident at an early gig.

There was one incident when The Slits were playing the same evening as us. Ari Up was quite mischievous, she couldn't have been more than fourteen or fifteen. Poly took her performances seriously, and of course she threw everything into it, so Ari Up pulled the electricity so that Poly's mike wasn't working when she started singing. That was a conscious act. There was this punky rivalry between the two. Poly was furious! It wasn't all love 'n' peace between the bands.

The Slits appeared in *The Punk Rock Movie,* but perhaps the most notable early recording was their first John Peel Session, enshrined on magnetic tape in 1977. Peel had remarked to friends that he wanted to see the band, and in due course, on 15 August at the Vortex Club, he did. An encounter with Palmolive resulted in him having his head knocked against that of the man standing next to him, but Peel and his lugubrious producer John Walters remained keen on the band, to the extent of arranging the 1977 session. Walters later remarked that despite their lack of musicality the band should be "recorded for posterity."

In September 1977 the band recorded this notable session, which ran to four tracks: *Love & Romance, Vindictive, New Town* and *Shoplifting.* The music was as raw and chaotic as any in punk, with Albertine herself impressed by the band's sheer energy. BBC engineer Nicholas Gomm had to retune their guitars every now and again since the band itself could not manage that basic procedure, but such was the essence of punk: don't worry about the technicalities, just get out there and do what needs to be done. This quartet of women had a lot to say and manifested aunique power in the saying. But there were detractors, including cynics at the BBC. Peel and Walters, meanwhile, attending the recordings without revealing their presence, fell about laughing as producers Tony Wilson and Bill Aiken struggled to extract anything useable from the untamed sonic volcano in their midst. Yet John Peel was no fool when it came to music and its place in cultural history. Something about The Slits spoke to him, and he would later remember the session and its 1978 counterpart as amongst the best he ever broadcast. That 1977 session alone was repeated six times in later editions of his radio programme.

This band was way ahead of the curve. Very few all-women bands had appeared, let alone achieved success in that male-dominated world of the 1970s music biz. Punk, with its D.I.Y. ethic and insistence on action not thinking about action, demanded that this group of four young women get out there and perform. Which they did; with ramshackle style, with untameable energy, and with a political nous superior to many in the movement. Like their allies The Clash, their music had a powerful and relevant message. Iconic punk women were as numerous as men: Viv Albertine and Ari Up, Poly Styrene and Lora Logic, Siouxsie Sioux. This was the beginning of a levelling up overdue for millennia, with punk a revolution that, for once, did reach out to the female half of the population. Women were finding their voices and staking out their places. The best of those women were hacking away in order to build *new* places. To quote Mary Beard: *If women are not perceived to be fully within the structures of power, surely it is power that we need to redefine rather than women?*

All the great women who appeared during the punk explosion went on to become individuals of character; distinctive, courageous, speaking their minds, being themselves. It was not just Viv Albertine who carved out a notable career and life after the first incarnation of The Slits fragmented. Alongside her were Siouxsie Sioux and Poly Styrene. And there were others, perhaps not so well known now but with as important a contribution: Lora Logic, Chrissie Hynde, Pauline Murray, Debbie Harry, Patti Smith, Ana da Silva. Da Silva was herself inspired to start a band (The Raincoats) when she saw The Slits on stage early in 1977.

Punk was a movement for *everybody:* men and women. This remains one of its most important legacies. Punk can claim to have changed society at its roots – a truly radical movement. And because plenty of work still needs to be done, punk retains its relevance to women in societies still wedded to the patriarchal template. Punk was not and is not male.

Chapter 17

She Ain't No Human Being

Why must we have kings and queens? It is a question many philosophers, sociologists, and even a few psychologists and anthropologists have asked. Some replies bang on about divine choice, divine right, the natural order of things, destiny and so forth; others talk of symbolism, tourism and other concepts. A few nations have dispensed with their monarchs altogether – Europe now has only a few neutered kings and queens, with a few acting to slim down their royal families to minimum size. Britain, for some reason, never followed such a path. When John Lydon found himself staring Queen Elizabeth's silver jubilee in the face, he scowled, for he did not like what he saw. There, he thought, in the coming summer of 1977, was an opportunity for mayhem, protest, and the ultimate revolution. Malcolm McLaren agreed. Together they would tell the British people the truth about their precious royal symbol.

God Save The Queen is a song like few others in the history of rock music. Not only was it deeply shocking in 1977, it used language that annihilated British tradition, satirised a living symbol who by convention could not answer back, and did all this in an iconic record sleeve with relish and panache. No punches were pulled. No prisoner was taken. This was an attempt at cultural assassination: regicide by punk. As a consequence, it is one of the most gloriously inventive, socially explosive singles ever released.

The British nation is one whose class system has caused it to become a stratified, unwieldy, inflexible hulk, dining out on nobility in stately homes, on the ownership of land and inherited wealth, and on laws protecting property and institutional rights. Britain exists as a mass society shaped as a pyramid hierarchy, with a large number at the bottom and increasingly few at the top. Its rules of elitism are unwritten, a convention allowing the continuation of the rights of the rich and privileged to continue as if they were perfectly natural. But they are not. As Tony Benn, that insightful man of wisdom remarked in one of the most widely shared memes on social media: *I don't think people realise how the establishment became established. They simply stole the land and property off the poor, surrounded themselves with weak minded sycophants for protection, gave themselves titles, and have been wielding power ever since.*

But a hierarchy needs a paramount symbol to manifest national concepts, to suck up to, and to represent the hearts and minds of that part of the nation allowed by the elite to be visible – themselves, in essence. A hierarchy as obdurate and narcissistic as the British one needs a special symbol. Such a symbol is the royal family. It is no accident that as the Enlightenment covered continental Europe with its notions of egality, fraternity and liberty, more sensible nations chose to remove their royal families for the sake of human decency. Britain never quite managed that feat. The British nation was too wedded to royal glory, to hope derived from the efforts of the ruling class, and to the idea of a permanent, unyielding social order in which some people were born into stately homes and others into council estates. This was the British way, unspoken because the elite deemed themselves intrinsically worth it. That was "obvious" and "self-evident."

Here lies a deep difference between Britain and its child America. In Britain, the European tradition of some individuals possessing intrinsic qualities – majesty, genius, charisma, destiny – remains at the heart of perceptions about the human condition. Paul McCartney, for instance, is the greatest melodist since Mozart because some genetic accident of his brain and therefore his mind make him exceptional even over the scope of centuries. This can be stated as a fact beyond reasonable doubt. An American would find the statement problematic, however. The American Dream, they would say, states that any individual can find such success as McCartney through sheer hard work. There is no intrinsic quality in people making them better than others.

The American position is incorrect because it ignores random acts and chance out there in the real world. It presumes as an article of irrational faith that reality defers to us – that hard work alone really can change everything, as opposed to a little. The truth is the reverse: *we* defer to *it,* to the real world and to its laws of chance. The European position, while correct, nevertheless takes biological truth and spreads its metaphorical influence everywhere. If Paul McCartney is a melodic genius because he was born that way, such a thing must apply elsewhere, in which case there is a "natural order" separating one individual from others and placing them in a stratified location. Yet, although the biology is correct and true, its application by a ruling elite is utterly selfish. Human beings can be either Paul McCartney or John Lydon and expect the same basic level of human decency: the right to free speech, the right to make a living and so on. That only Paul McCartney and no other could write songs like *Yesterday, Maybe I'm Amazed* or *Band On The Run* in no way detracts either from the achievements of Lydon and the Pistols, or from humanity in general. Everyone is different, with some people brilliant beyond the norm; but we are nonetheless entitled to the same level of egality, fraternity and liberty. Biology is not destiny. Nobility is not biology. Elitism is not noble.

This misapplication of the concept of individual specialness lies at the heart both of royalty and the entire class system. Both are deeply narcissistic concepts. When John Lydon came to write the lyrics for *God Save The Queen,* he sensed the profound selfishness of the institution of monarchy, its ability to preserve itself through the application of unspoken social norms held only by the elite, and its social unjustness. Royalty, he perceived, was deeply discriminatory – and he knew he was living on the underside of that social institution.

The song was at first called *No Future,* and various members of the band stated afterwards that it was not originally intended as an anti-monarchy diatribe. With music written by Glen Matlock (already ejected from the band for liking The Beatles), it was an evocation of the misery of the British working classes, simultaneously looking up at their supposed betters while being mistreated by them. It spoke truth to undeserved, institutional power.

The opening couplet of the song was about as traumatic for the British nation as they could have imagined: *God save the Queen, the fascist regime.* 1976 was just three decades on from the end of the Second World War, at a time when the majority of the British population had either served themselves or had personal memories of the conflict. To describe royalty, who would have been perceived by most of the populace as an institution who had helped to save Britain against Germany, as fascist was as vitriolic a piece of imagery as Lydon could have written, intended with wit and derision to inflict the maximum amount of pain. Moreover, it co-opted into its opening phrase the opening line from the cherished national anthem: double the pain. Nothing was spared here. Punk's attitude to every absurdity, injustice, fraud and prejudice of the establishment, be they monarch, elite or upper classes, was there for all to see.

The next couplet almost matched the opener for shock value. Now Lydon turned his attention to those who celebrate monarchy, telling them that they had been turned into morons – potential H-bombs, no less. Here, however, he could have been talking to anybody in Britain, including members of his own social class, much as he did on *So It Goes* when he challenged the audience to "get off their arse." The British, he observed, were infantilised by monarchy, made into simpering flag wavers lacking any critical faculty, who chuckled, bowed and scraped before their supposed betters. The line was utterly without guile: a simple statement of fact in language relevant to the 1970s.

A third shock line followed, made more devastating by the target it aimed at: the Queen herself. *She ain't no human being.* Hearing those five words would have made every supporter of monarchy at once furious and petrified. It was a martial declaration of scorn in terms as malicious as possible – genius or treachery, depending on your stance. Lydon went on to describe the nation's royal road as meaningless: *There is no future in England's dreaming.* Our traditions were nothing more than dreams, he stated, pleasant, sunlit, and lacking any justice or egality.

The next couplet was more of a plea to those who saw things the way he did. He urged his listeners not to be told what they wanted, not to be told what they needed. As in the songs of Poly Styrene, these lines took a swipe at the prevailing situation in which infantilised consumers suckled at the teat of consumerism, made attractive by an advertising industry which in any theatre other than commerce would be ruled inhumane and dangerous. But it also applied to valueless jobs for working class people, an education system based on the nineteenth century factory model which aimed only to make competent employees, and a social system which penalised the poor for their lack of ready cash: *No future for you.*

The next verse included one of Lydon's most brilliant lines: *We mean it, maaaan.* If sarcasm was a substance, it would be the poison dripping from these four words. An equivalent dose followed: *We love our queen, god saves.* And when Lydon sang these lyrics he used all the mockery he could muster via his extraordinary diction – a tour de force. Further scorn followed, that the nation's figurehead was not what she seemed… *God save history, god save your mad parade…* He concluded by asking how there could be sin if there was no future.

The song concluded with its depressing, disillusioned chant: *No future for you…* Lydon *meant* all this. He had had enough of what he had seen. He wanted to lash out, destroy, ruin, then get pissed in the wreckage he had created. It was a truly noble aim, if that word is used in its proper sense – exhibiting high personal qualities or ethical principles. For this song in the band's canon made a *moral* case, that royalty was an empty, divisive, inhumane institution, that those who lauded it were blinded by the light shining out of the Windsor's arses, and that he, Johnny Rotten of the Sex Pistols, had the right, the intelligence and the opportunity to make his case for the sake of the country he lived in.

The single was released on Virgin Records on 27 May 1977, shortly before the culmination of various silver jubilee celebrations planned or undertaken after the official date of 6 February. Dates in June had been set aside for events, and Malcolm McLaren was not going to miss the opportunity to scorn, satirise and outshine the royal pageant of jubilee week. Some of the events were national – tea parties for children, for instance – while others were based in London and were due to attract much media interest. At one tea party in deepest rural Shropshire a callow youth attended, enjoying the excitement and following the trend for adulation, little knowing that forty-seven years later he would write a book from the other side of the fence.

One event in particular caught the gaze of McLaren and the Pistols. On 9 June, the Queen intended making a trip along the River Thames. This, McLaren realised, was something well worth mocking, something which might catapult the single up the charts. All publicity was good publicity. So he arranged for the Sex Pistols to make an equivalent voyage, satirising the royal event with full, sarcastic intent. The vessel was chartered privately and with the full support of Virgin Records, who had signed the band after they were dumped by the petrified A&M record label, who had been attempting to haul them up following the departure from EMI. Richard

Branson knew the value of the band, and decided to financially support their river trip and ensure it was licenced. The idea was that the band would perform their music, not least the offending 45, while the vessel passed the various ancient buildings and historic monuments of the capital city. Julian Temple was on hand to film events.

There was plenty of publicity, but McLaren's plan did not go as he expected. Police officers also on the river forced the vessel to dock, their foam-flecked launches barring the way, while officers and backup policemen on the riverbank surrounded Westminster Pier. As fast as possible, the band, McLaren and Vivienne Westwood were spirited away, soon to be arrested alongside other Pistols aides and supporters, including soon-to-be PiL bassist Jah Wobble. The attempt had been made, then stopped in the full glare of media publicity. As far as McLaren could see, that was perfect.

Branson himself argued with the police, explaining that they had acquired the correct licence and abided by the standard terms. Yet, aware of the potential for publicity of the same intensity as the Grundy affair six months earlier, he observed it all, letting events take their natural course. He knew what positive consequences might follow from the "debacle."

Head of Virgin Records A&R Simon Draper was on the infamous boat the *MV Queen Elizabeth* that day.

> *It was a typical Thames riverboat. We set off from Charing Cross Pier early in the evening. The band were on board, Richard Branson too, and they began to play their music. It was loud. I remember Adam Ant – Stuart Goddard as he was then – was also with us, dressed up in a semi-bondage outfit. He looked dark and charismatic, and was rather voluble. But then the police began to follow us in their own boats. They stopped us eventually, and ordered us back to base. Malcolm attempted to get himself arrested – he did find himself in a cell later. Richard didn't do anything like that. He was supportive of such stunts – he loved them. He thought it was ridiculous of the police to stop this particular stunt, when there was no real reason for them to turn up. But there was a widespread feeling at the time that the Sex Pistols were dangerous. I suppose that supplied their motive.*

As it happened, the consequences of the 45's release did not include reaching the top of the charts. Although even today nothing can be proven one way or the other, there is evidence suggesting that the British Phonograph Institute removed sales of singles from record company owned shops (such as the Virgin Megastore in Oxford Street) during jubilee week. That meant *God Save The Queen* did not hit number one, instead peaking one place down, behind Rod Stewart. Meanwhile, the BBC placed a total ban on playing the song, a stance followed by the Independent Broadcasting Authority. In addition, various high street stockists refused to carry the single, including the then prominent WH Smith, and Woolworths. Indeed, in WH Smith stores the number 2 chart position was replaced with an empty space. Establishment censors were busy censoring.

There were other, more unpleasant consequences. Much of the British public felt offended by the song, and when Lydon and the single's producers were caught outside a Highbury pub they were attacked, and injured with razor blades. This incident further fanned the flames of publicity, placing McLaren, Lydon and the band at the centre of a media storm.

But it was not just the music, the media furore and the band's notoriety which rankled. Even the artwork was controversial.

When released as a 45 by Virgin Records, the song was housed in a 7" cardboard square designed by Jamie Reid, which has gone down over the years as a punk icon; one often named as the greatest single cover ever. It depicted Cecil Beaton's photograph of Queen Elizabeth II against a blue background, her mouth and eyes covered with the newsprint styled typography for which Reid at the time was famous, and which would go on to grace the band's only LP. Reid was a bit of a Renaissance man, an artist, a peace and socialism activist, an anarchist and a supporter of the punk movement, who had a decisive impact on it. He too was subject to the violent undercurrents of the time. Attacked for wearing a T shirt depicting the *God Save The Queen* cover art, he was hospitalised. Pressing plant employees, meanwhile, refused to print the sleeve, causing further scandal and upheaval.

Reid's classic punk art style emerged from his activism during the previous decade, when poverty stopped him from using the standard tools of the artist's trade. Appropriating and using newspaper text was far cheaper than buying printing equipment. In this way, more by accident than any considered artistic ethic, he single-handedly defined a great part of the look of punk, its ominous collages and cut-up photomontages manifesting its D.I.Y., ad hoc ethos.

Reid had been a friend of Malcolm McLaren at the art school they both attended, and it was not long before he was enthusiastically designing other images for the band – singles and the LP. Soon, his style was everywhere. Further royal images gave the Queen a safety pin as adornment, and placed her against a defaced, tattered Union Jack. As intended, it led to maximum outrage.

That sense of public disbelief, resentment and anger would be intensified when later in 1977 the band released their long-playing final statement: *Never Mind The Bollocks, Here's The Sex Pistols.*

Chapter 18

Bollocks

The album's title was coined by guitarist Steve Jones, the phrase resonating with him and the others of the band: never mind the nonsense. Released on 28 October 1977 by Virgin Records, it burst through what remained of the 1970s musical haze in a fist-fight of ferocious, sneering fury. It caused as much of a stink as *God Save The Queen,* and was censored, banned, and generally messed around with by various self-appointed guardians of the establishment. But Richard Branson, who possessed as cunning a sense of publicity as the band's manager, supported the album through all its obstacles and dramas. There would be quite a few of those.

The album comprised twelve tracks, recorded on various occasions through the year, with Bill Price and Chris Thomas producing and engineering the recordings. It opened with a classic descending guitar chord sequence leading into the LP's advance single, *Holidays In The Sun.* This song reached number eight in the charts – a respectable position, given the media furore of the time. There was the hint of a hangover from glam rock in the stomping feet and guitar style; an uneasy echo of Gary Glitter mixed with jackboots. Written about a fortnight in Berlin spent escaping threats and adversity in London, the song was punchy and lyrically astute, celebrating the absurdity of the split city and its unmistakeable symbol, the Berlin Wall. Lydon's vocals for this opening cut were both ferocious and politically aware, as he chanted *I gotta go over the wall, I wanna go over the Berlin Wall* while the song played out, this verbal torrent a perfect example of his gift for speaking musically. He had received a positive impression of the city, despite its schizoid geography and the knowledge that East Berliners – themselves captives under threat in a major city – looked to the decadent, consumerist West for inspiration and hope. The irony of this was not lost on him.

Bodies was more of a visceral shocker, a depiction of the reality of abortion in seventies Britain only a decade after Liberal MP David Steel managed to get the archaic British law updated via his private member's bill. The song was inspired by one of the mentally damaged fans who followed the band, a young woman called Pauline, well known on the circuit, often feared, sometimes dangerous. She was thought to be in and out of a mental institute. The opening lines described her chaotic life with precision: *She was a girl from Birmingham, she just had an abortion.* The song ended in a splenetic burst of fuck and fucking, accentuating the horror of Pauline's circumstances, the more so as the lyrics then played out on the repeated refrain, *Body, I'm not an animal.* Difficult listening to this day.

The third cut was *No Feelings,* a song about selfishness. Based around a fast Steve Jones riff, the song was one of very few in the band's repertoire whose tempo brought on breathlessness. The lyrics were again sparse and brutal. *Liar* was a forthright denunciation written by Matlock and Lydon of anybody in the band's entourage or elsewhere in their sights who refused to tell them the truth. By the time of the LP's release, that included Malcolm McLaren, as well as the standard array of politicians and other members of the despised British establishment.

The fifth track was already well known to the album's feverish buyers: *God Save The Queen.* It roused the listener as the band rampaged through the music at the end of the LP's A side. *Problems* was more of a complex cut, albeit that it began after a band jam troubled by creative exhaustion. This song cohered once the bass riff and drum parts were settled, its spontaneity matching its lyrical back-and-forth: *And I can see there's something wrong with you... Don't come to me if you need pity.* Later in the song the imagery is particularly visceral: *Eat your heart out on a plastic tray, you don't do what you want and you'll fade away.*

The B side opened with *Seventeen,* a song about the typical life of a teenager. All the members of the band had struggled with the tedium, lack of opportunity and hope, and sense of urban imprisonment of their lives, and the song depicted that situation. Boredom and disillusionment were shot through with ennui and carelessness. Although writing had been initiated by Jones, Lydon's lyrics were far more powerful than the originals; they stayed. *You're only twenty-nine, got a lot to learn, but when your mummy dies, she will not return.* He flailed out at those around him too: *We don't care about long hair, I don't wear flares.* (Flared trousers were an essential fashion statement through the first half of the 1970s.)

Following on came the band's debut single, *Anarchy In The U.K.*, which retained all its glorious ability to shock. *Submission* however was more of an oddity, and the only song to feature any sort of audio other than drums, bass, guitars and vocals. Another Matlock/Lydon dual creation, it was a piss-take of the band's manager trying to direct the creative flow, with Lydon remaking the word submission into submarine mission. *I can't figure out your watery love, I got to solve your mystery.* The song seemed a little out of place both musically and lyrically alongside the other eleven tracks, though it just about managed to keep the LP going as the end came into view.

Pretty Vacant in due course became a third storming single, opening with another classic Steve Jones riff, adapted, according to Matlock who wrote the song, from the piano part in Abba's *SOS.* This does sound unlikely, but Abba were an omnipresent phenomenon at the time, inspiring other songwriters such as Elvis Costello to mimic melodic fragments. As an exercise in crowbarring the word cunt into a song it succeeded, but it was also one of the best tunes on the album and had the best chord sequence, toughened up by Jones' apocalyptic chorused guitars (both he and drummer Cook were studio devotees). The lyrics were an ear-splitting warning of immediate, if unspecified action, a cry for recognition as much as one for action, in an era of union dominance, political uncertainty, and hardship for the working class. *I don't believe illusions, too much is real, stuff your cheap comment… 'cos we know what we feel.* Most kids felt like this, the litter on the streets through which they kicked their way an obvious symptom of damage and discontent. Beneath flickering sodium lamps, those kids wrung what sustenance they could out of the washrags of life.

New York was another band reaction to their increasingly insufferable manager, this time his ever-mutating tales of days spent in the New York scene. Lydon demolished him and his prattling with concise, cutting lyrics: *You better keep your mouth shut, you're in a rut. Kiss this,* the closing lyric, later became another band phrase used with success well after its sell-by date.

The album closer was *EMI,* a song written to mock the band's former record label. It was ferocious and direct: *I tell you it was all a frame, they only did it 'cos of fame.* This had been the way of it as the global corporation got its fingers burned with what they took to be a manageable, if shocking, musical unit. But the Pistols cared nothing for appearances, for spending the forty grand, or for any consequences of their departure. The hype and the violence surrounding their gigs and their personal lives were becoming unbearable, and band friction, notably between Matlock and Lydon in the early days, was beginning to spiral out of control. A year earlier, the band had in a haze of optimism signed with EMI and recorded demo versions and then the final version of their debut single. Now, as a failing October began to hint at winter, the end was nigh.

A flurry of activity accompanied the final preparations for the album's release, with Branson deciding which tracks and which mixes of those tracks to include. Matters were not helped by the appearance of a bootleg LP of earlier song versions, entitled *Spunk* and of unknown origin. There was also a French edition with a slightly different track list to contend with. In the end the LP was rush-released with the band's four singles all included, a decision which did not recommend itself either to the band or their manager. But Branson, who when he started in the music business achieved success through importing LPs into Britain, felt he had little choice under the circumstances.

Anticipation was intense. Advance orders topped a hundred thousand. After a week of sales the LP reached number one in the album charts – no small achievement given that most chain retailers refused to stock it.

Although Glen Matlock was listed on the release as one of the four songwriters – he had contributed to the writing of almost every song during 1975 – by the time the album was into the early stages of recording he had been booted out and replaced with the much more dangerous, self-destructive and punk-looking Sid Vicious. By the end of February 1977, Vicious was a fixture in the band. However, he was still in the early stages of learning bass guitar, his lack of ability covered by Steve Jones taking on the lion's share of the bass duties. In fact Matlock had been asked to return to play bass owing to these woeful recordings, but he refused when no up-front cash appeared. Such problems, technical difficulties (various mixes were to be merged on some songs), and the increasing sense of a band beginning to tear itself apart, contributed to the chaotic splendour of the LP, which despite all the problems managed to rip through the nation's airwaves and eardrums. The guitars in particular sounded awesome, with Lydon proving himself to be one of rock's great vocalists, his half sung, half-spoken style and exaggerated diction a unique feature of the music. It was a shocker and a classic, a definitive statement of a whirlwind year. It both marked the punk explosion, epitomised it, and acted as the sound at the beginning of the end.

The cover was also a classic. Jamie Reid's minimal design in dayglo yellow and flesh-tone pink used typography and cut-out print to broadcast its stark message. Nothing like it had been seen before, most LPs using photographs of the artist or band, painted images, or exotic concoctions assembled and photographed by design studios such as Hypgnosis, whose work for the enemy group Pink Floyd was legendary even in 1977.

The album's critical reception by music journalists was positive. It was viewed as lightning from a stormy sky. The general media scrum around the band intensified, however, making Lydon in particular feel uncomfortable. The band's reputation had been stoked up in part by McLaren through deliberate acts of provocation, and now they were all finding success, but having to cope with the sometimes violent consequences of that blaze of publicity. They had ridiculed the establishment in all its forms. Now, there was kickback.

Censorship of record shop advertisement posters continued to cause controversy, with the police getting involved. It seems strange now, in times of expletive-filled broadcasting, but the word *bollocks* was problematic to some in 1977. To the high and mighty of the establishment that word epitomised the insolence of the band and its manager. They would therefore have to be dealt with.

The court case was bizarre. Christopher Seale was a Virgin Records retail manager in Nottingham, who had displayed the LP and its accompanying poster in his shop window. Warned that the word bollocks on LP and poster was offensive, he was arrested under the Indecent Advertisements Act, a British statute going back to Victorian times. This was reported with glee and relish by the press afterwards. But Seale stood his ground, continuing to offer promotion and sale of the LP; and he had supporters. Not only were the music press on his side, Branson himself weighed in. There can be little doubt that publicity was at the back of Branson's mind when he acted as he did, but to pay for legal costs and employ none other than

John Mortimer – he of the *Oz* magazine obscenity trial, the blasphemous libel suit aimed at the editor of *Gay News,* and many others – was a deed of some courage.

The obscenity case, consisting of four charges, came to court on 24 November, less than a month after the album's release. It had all the characteristics of a very British farce. Mortimer was quick to point out that the word in question was only taken to be obscene when presented by the Sex Pistols and their commercial associates, and that when the word was used elsewhere – for instance by the press – there was no difficulty. This, in his view, was simple discrimination enacted by the police. It was a matter of hypocrisy: a classic British double standard.

Mortimer had an ace up his sleeve which took events further into farce. Calling Professor James Kinsley to the witness stand from his abode at the local university, he proceeded to demonstrate with this academic's help that the work bollock in English was a perfectly acceptable term meaning a priest. In the case of the LP, it was argued, that term clearly meant nonsense – the original sense of Steve Jones' original, off-the-cuff remark which caused the album to be renamed.

With considerable reluctance, as demonstrated by the verbiage in which the judgement was housed, the chairman of the court found the defendants not guilty on all charges, remarking that the use of such vulgarity for the purposes of commercial gain was deplorable.

The Sex Pistols achieved much during the year of punk. From their renaming late in 1975, through the chaos, strife, hope and expectations of 1976 alongside many others of the punk movement, the band in 1977 navigated constant abuse, discrimination and attempted legal proceedings by the establishment, and the vitriol and violence of a large portion of the British public. They were loathed by mass media and adored by the music press. They were hated and loved. They had their fans, their followers, a stack of cash, and that satisfaction induced by releasing one of the great rock albums. But now such things were beginning to wear thin.

An eight-date Never Mind The Bans Tour was scheduled for December, but outside pressures and illness halved that. Exhaustion was beginning to set in. Christmas Day, when they played in Huddersfield, would be their final British appearance in this form.

Chapter 19

Everybody's On Top Of The Pops

Few media organisations in the world match the British Broadcasting Corporation. Established by the government and with a royal charter, its reach, stature and heritage made its position until the arrival of streaming and the internet unassailable. It still stands alone amongst similar organisations, the oldest and largest public service broadcaster in the world.

With extensive television and radio arms, the BBC came to dominate British cultural life in a unique manner, not least in the field of music. Radios 2, 3 and 4 grew out of earlier national services, with Radio 1 a late response to youth culture and the allure of offshore pirate stations. Popular music on television was limited, often limp or patronising, until the rise of BBC1's premier music programme *Top Of The Pops.* Instituted on New Year's Day 1964, it was a charts-based programme that came to dominate the nation's pop, and later rock music viewing. At the outset artistes and groups mimed to their chart hits, but that soon changed after action by the Musicians' Union. Soon, a novel mode of operation was in place, where performers would re-record their music to backing tapes that featured BBC musicians. This was deemed acceptable for while, until the arrival (at the time daring and controversial) of live performances. But in 1976, when punk burst onto the scene, the BBC faced a dilemma.

They banned various classic punk singles, notably those by the Sex Pistols. While this gave the band publicity in newspapers, it also acted against them, as their music reached a smaller audience than it could have. Gigs and vinyl were all very well, but national exposure on the airwaves was vital. As for *Top Of The Pops*… how could the BBC possibly allow a punk band to appear? At the time, it seemed impossible to conceive.

Up in Scotland meanwhile, a band called The Rezillos formed in 1976, and although more of a happy-go-lucky outfit without the intensity of some punk bands, they were much influenced by what was happening in

London and across the nation. After signing up for their debut LP, they wrote and recorded a song which would go down as both a classic 45 and an ironic comment on the BBC's flagship pop programme.

It was called *Everybody's On Top Of The Pops.* The lyrics made the situation between the punk movement and the programme quite plain: *Does it matter what is shown, just as long as everyone knows… Take the money, leave the box, everybody's on top of the pops.* The catchy tune and the band's distinctive look made this a top twenty hit, though few can have missed the relevance of the message.

For the Rezillos, more influenced by beat music and US garage sounds, being a punk band – or, if not that, being labelled as one – did not conflict with appearing on Thursday evenings on prime-time television, to be watched and enjoyed by millions of young people. For them, *Top Of The Pops* was a natural, desirable outcome of their musical ambitions. But for other bands the situation was much more complex, and involved punk's ethical stance, its dismissal of established norms, its scorn of chart-based music, and its wish to connect with a living, breathing gig audience. For some bands, live music and their recorded output was the goal. *Top Of The Pops* must be rejected.

Of these bands, The Clash were the preeminent philosophers. They refused to play on the show on principle - a brave decision as that stance lost them sales and valuable exposure. But they were a band somehow both within and also outside the punk movement. They were the real thing, not a product of televisual entertainment, nor anything that such entertainment could exploit. As outsiders, they had the rare option of looking *into* the movement, seeing its pitfalls, avoiding its traps. *TOTP,* being part of that food chain, was seen by the band as an entertainment farce.

Another band of the time, The Skids, found themselves riven by dissent when the possibility came up of them appearing. On one side of the argument, Richard Jobson was in favour; Stuart Adamson was not. But even Jobson felt torn by what he was hearing from other quarters. Acquainted with members of the Sex Pistols, he was advised by them to do the show – it was publicity, after all. But Adamson still felt that ethical imperative: be true to your roots, be true to the principles of the punk movement.

Even if a band was accepted into the *TOTP* circle, there were still outdated attitudes to negotiate. A BBC producer could wield great power, to the extent of telling any band the limits to how they should present themselves. The BBC was a cultural monolith, and as such it could set a limit to the reality it presented. It felt it had the right to do that, enshrined in its charter.

Who the first punk band to appear on *Top Of The Pops* was is a matter of opinion, depending on what that opinion is of such bands. For a purist, it might be the Sex Pistols, for a generalist it might be The Jam. Like a number of the bands at the heart of this heterodox movement, The Jam were kind of punk but also had outside elements, in their case superb songs and Rickenbacker guitars echoing the 1960s. Paul Weller had the attitude and the underclass vision, but he was also a gifted songwriter with music in his blood. Some saw him as too good to be punk – too mod, in fact. But The Jam did play their single *In The City* on the show half way through May 1977, which gives them a shot at being the first punk band to be seen there. Their performance was imbued with all the energy and twisting power that they became famous for in later years, Weller spitting out his vocals, Foxton bouncing around the stage, Buckler providing the solid rhythm.

Although the Sex Pistols did not – could not – appear in person on the show, when their penultimate single *Pretty Vacant* was released they made a promotional film of them playing it, a film shown on *TOTP* that summer. Though they had lost none of their stage presence, something about that showing marked the beginning of the end. Vicious tried to look bored and aloof, while Lydon, wearing a long-sleeved *Destroy* shirt, snarled and ridiculed with his customary charisma. Their version of punk was a genuine underground movement which owed nothing to anyone. It was its own entity. So for the BBC to show the promotional film with its cunning wordplay from Lydon effectively boxed in the movement's heroes, making them a little more safe, a little more palatable. It was possible now to imagine the band and their music to be a commodity, albeit from a distance.

Another close call of that year came from The Adverts. Punk was nothing if not confrontational, and it sometimes had great intelligence behind it. The remarkable *Gary Gilmore's Eyes* was a hit single for the band in September 1977, describing what might happen to Gilmore's eyes (actually his corneas) after he had been executed by firing squad. Not only that, the song had a great tune. Gilmore, convicted of murder, had asked that suitable parts of his body be donated for transplant, or, if not, for scientific purposes. The case was widely reported upon as it played out. The Adverts got to perform their hit on *Top Of The Pops* knowing that the subject of their song had inspired a majestic, intoxicating 45.

Whether or not The Boomtown Rats were a punk band is a moot point. Opinions vary. Whatever the case, their debut single *Lookin' After No. 1* was sneery and supercharged enough to qualify in some minds, and the band appeared on *TOTP* in August 1977. The single made number eleven in Britain and scraped just under the top of the charts in their native Ireland. The band would go on to become a mainstay of the post-punk New Wave movement, with a string of hits to their name.

Most punk compilations feature *Do Anything You Wanna Do* by Eddie & the Hot Rods, an anthemic, unforgettable song released in July 1977. Forever a classic one-off, its striking melody and inspirational lyrics coupled with the band's unique look gave them a massive hit, with the single reaching number nine. Again, the song is not quite punk – more power-punk, or even power-pop – but Eddie & the Hot Rods were associated at the time with others of the punk movement. The band duly appeared on *TOTP* to promote their single.

Generation X, meanwhile, after a whirlwind of line-up changes and inter-band conflicts, managed to get onto the show in September 1977. But theirs was a controversial placement due to some punks calling them out as middle-class wannabes slumming it, others describing them and their music as empty, some saying they were too commercial or accessible to be true punks. None of this mattered to the band's front man Billy Idol, for whom all forms of publicity were to be attempted. The music press dismissed them as the established press and the BBC welcomed them – not for Idol or Generation X the ethical dilemmas facing Joe Strummer and Mick Jones.

As for those gifted musos The Stranglers, they had two 1977 hits to mime to on *TOTP, Go Buddy Go* and *No More Heroes,* the latter another epic punk anthem appearing on every compilation CD. On the show, Jean-Jacques Burnel hilariously tried to waft away the clouds of dry ice surrounding them while Hugh Cornwell applied himself to the song's withering lyrics. But he too messed around to his "rock god" guitar solo, while Dave Greenfield, resplendent in his trademark olive-hued jumpsuit, showed off just one of the reasons the band were streets ahead of the motley collection of zeroes accompanying them on that week's show. Their appearance for *Go Buddy Go* had them swap bass and guitar, giving Jean-Jacques Burnel the opportunity to display all the pent-up aggression he felt at the time, while Greenfield played a Hohner Cembalet solo at fractionally under the speed of light. The band were well on their way to stardom.

But it was perhaps a less well-known band, The Saints from Australia, who had the most punkish 45 to grace the *TOTP* studio around this time. *This Perfect Day* was an anthem jacked up on speed, a high octane roll through real punk territory. Released early in the summer of 1977, it charted relatively low despite its distinctive melody and drawled vocal delivery, but still earned the band a slot on *TOTP* introduced by Kid Jensen (a real music fan, unlike most of the Radio 1 DJs of the time). The song's lyrics were true to the ethos of the movement: *I've seen them drive around in cars, all look the same, get drunk in bars, and don't talk back, we got no social rights.* Its spirit of desperation lashed out at the listener: *Ain't nothing has changed it all goes on, and they'll keep laughing 'til the end.*

The BBC had for many years been at the heart of a broadcasting dilemma created by the monopoly they held over the nation's eyes and ears. In the 1970s they were at the centre of most households, and they knew that. They had a *duty*, enshrined in law, to provide for their audience. In the 1950s they had been taunted, satirised and needled by Spike Milligan, presiding genius of the Goons, to the extent that some of the high and mighty within their ranks tried to get the show removed from the airwaves. An intervention by announcer John Snagge – then perceived as BBC nobility – ensured the show was saved, and it went on to become immensely popular, not to mention influential and beloved across the country, as it is to this day. The British audience *wanted* the Goons, whatever the upper echelons of the corporation thought of them. A similar situation applied to the punk explosion. The BBC had to reflect the nation's interests and choices, regardless of what they themselves thought. On their flagship pop music programme they were required to show what was going on up and down the charts, whether that be light, heavy, throwaway ditty or protest song.

Faced with punk, they had to steer a path between censoring lyrics they deemed offensive – a stipulation of the law – and presenting the snotty-nosed, hundred-mile-per-hour truth of the movement. They were chaps in suits and bowler hats, while the luminaries of punk were not. That abyss had to be bridged. As the punk volcano sputtered and showed signs of ceasing its explosive activity, they dipped their toes into the A-bombed arena and reflected what they could of it. Anarchy, anger, adrenaline. That reflection included Johnny Rotten in his *Destroy* shirt on *Top Of The Pops.* As the carefully typed memos of the time might have said: it simply had to be done.

Chapter 20

White Riot

They were punk's conscience: no nonsense, no compromise, no surrender. The Clash were there at the beginning, their members having lived under the names The 101ers and London SS, bands playing in London before punk rock broke cover. Joe Strummer (real name John Graham Mellor) and Mick Jones were in those two bands, the latter combo seeing a few punk luminaries pass through its ranks, including soon-to-be Clash member Topper Headon. One other Clash fixture auditioned for London SS but did not make the cut: bass player Paul Simonon.

London SS were managed by Bernie Rhodes, an acquaintance of Malcolm McLaren, so it was not long before the Pistols and The Clash got to know one another. With London SS going defunct early in 1976, the ground was laid for Mick Jones, having watched the Pistols at one of their earliest gigs, to be amazed and energised by proto-punk energy, not to mention its potential for fear and loathing. He saw the light. He grasped at once that something was changing in London's music scene, that a baton was about to be passed from the old order to the new. Bernie Rhodes then paved the way for the first incarnation of The Clash to arrive, including Joe Strummer on lead vocals, a man and a performer everybody had been impressed with upon meeting. Drummer Terry Chimes briefly worked with the band before Headon arrived. In due course, the classic line up was ready to rock: Strummer, Jones, Simonon and Headon.

Joe Strummer had also been inspired and energised by seeing the Sex Pistols, who supported The 101ers on one of their pub rock dates. Strummer at once realised his band, style and music were about to expire. Like so many in London at the time who saw the Pistols in their raw, untamed, ferocious youth, he was transformed. This was music carrying an energy which could bring a revolution.

That revolution as far as The Clash were concerned began on 4 July, when the band supported the Sex Pistols at a Sheffield gig. But with early guitarist Keith Levene already uncomfortable in the band, and with a lack of cohesion to their musical presence, it seemed time for a rethink. In the meantime, both bands plus many other punk luminaries attended the second British appearance by The Ramones at Dingwalls, an event which provided further inspiration. Strummer in particular was enthused by that band's debut LP, which, alongside their appearance in Britain, gave him and the nascent punk movement an early shot of conceptual caffeine.

Bernie Rhodes was no wallflower when it came to management. Perceiving that his band were somewhat lacking in comparison with their peers, he insisted they tighten up their act, holding them back from gigs until they were ready. But in Joe Strummer he had a willing pupil, both men recognising the Year Zero qualities of the punk movement, in which everything from before had to be ditched. But they *liked* that. They banished the old order from their lives and gratefully, enthusiastically and without dissent embrace the new. The Clash had to stand out, had to express a punk manifesto through their music and their artistic choices, had to set themselves apart in order to be noticed. That was the new deal.

Then everything fell into place for the classic version of the band. Strummer was a gifted lyricist and Mick Jones could set it all to music. As the intensity of the band's operations increased within this new template, as punk exploded, and as their own confidence increased, they began to write about the problems of their lives and of the society they lived in. They were not a nostalgic band, not a sentimental band: they were a band of thinkers, of doers. They were *active.* They wrote about the circumstances of their lives as, day by day, they lived them.

Strummer and Jones were the obvious front of stage force, but the band as a whole was a powerful unit. At a private gig that summer, music press journalists found themselves struck by the band's passion, intensity and power. This looked like another iconic group in punk's glittering array.

Two weeks later, at another seminal London gig, they, the Sex Pistols and Buzzcocks comprised a triple bill of titanic proportions, further cementing the importance of the punk movement, which at the time still had three months to run before its Grundy moment. Yet in London in particular, the word was spreading. Punk was going to destroy the old order. The Clash, Sex Pistols, The Vibrators, Eater, The Stranglers, Chelsea, The Damned, Buzzcocks… these bands and more *were* going to bring a revolution.

The Clash spoke without restraint about the issues their songs highlighted. They were lefties, they were social agitators and commentators, they were anti-racism, and they wanted to inspire a downtrodden, numbed youth. Uncomfortable with punk's nihilistic streak, they promoted the active stance of individuals, that everyone could stand up for themselves and make a difference, not only to their own lives but to the lives of others.

Standing up against that racism endemic to conservative British society and elsewhere in the former colonialist country, the band wrote about injustices present as a consequence of misdeeds undertaken by a nation which had once been at the centre of a blood-spattered empire. At the Notting Hill Carnival of that year, when black youths found themselves pitted against white police, violence spoiled the event, leaving a bitter taste in everybody's mouth. Strummer found himself both appalled and inspired. As a consequence, he wrote the lyrics to the band's debut 45, the two-minute *White Riot,* to which Jones provided the music.

Yet far too many people misinterpreted this classic of the punk canon, released as the year of punk, 1977, began to flower, and to his annoyance Strummer found himself having to defend the band against accusations of racism. *White Riot,* he explained, was about white youth fighting injustice and violence just as black youth was doing. The song was intended to inspire, to sound the battle cry, to mobilise white young people in the same struggle being undertaken by less fortunate and entitled groups. White youth in London could observe an over-zealous, institutionally racist police force perpetrating unjust operations across the capital against black youth. It was up to them to join the fray, that such injustices be exposed, resisted, and in due course be concluded via the processes of law. The single went on to scrape the bottom of the charts, peaking at number 38. In terms of its critical reception, however, and its eventual place in punk rock history, it was a number 1 hit. Most of the music press journalists who reviewed it saw it in the same light as they saw the Pistols' debut a few months earlier: colossal, significant, ferocious, profound. *White Riot* was a game-changer.

So was the debut LP, released the following month. That was a number 12 smash. Punk was here to speak truth to power via *The Clash,* to break the foundation stones of the establishment, to encourage all alienated and bored young people to go out and stand up for what they believed in. Yes, there were differing opinions on the band signing a relatively high-earning deal with CBS Records. Mark Perry of *Sniffin' Glue* fanzine was not impressed. CBS, however, were devoted to the band, and supported them in various ways. Doubtless this irony of the band's early existence was not lost on Strummer & co.

The band would go on to play various Rock Against Racism benefit gigs. Author Jon Courtenay Grimwood attended an early such event.

> *There's safety in numbers, which is just as well given the skinheads crowding every corner of London's East End, who make no secret of wanting to kick our heads in. And the officers from the Met who are policing this march have made their loyalties clear, and it's not with the punks and rastas and rude boys with our Anti-Nazi League placards and Rock Against Racism badges. We're moving through National Front central and frankly I'm terrified. But no-one else on the march looks afraid so I sneer and throw insults back and try to work out if I can still hear Misty in Roots. They're somewhere ahead, playing from the back of a truck.*
>
> *There are a hundred thousand of us heading the six miles from Trafalgar Square to Victoria Park, where the Clash will headline.*
>
> *But it's Poly Styrene from X Ray Specs I remember. She's in your face, barely in tune, fired up on where she is and why, and we respond, at least the section of crowd I'm in does. We pogo, mouth the words, pump our fists as guitar and bass and drums batter us, and Poly's scream washes over us, vicious enough to melt metal. It's a young crowd. A furious crowd. In that moment we believe we can make the difference. We believe this matters.*

The White Riot Tour took place in May 1977. It was intended to take punk out of the capital city and into parts of the country that had only seen punk in print. The Clash stood at the head of a barrage of punk talent, including The Jam, Buzzcocks, The Slits, Subway Sect and The Prefects.

The tour's opening night at the Roxy Club featured three of the titans of the movement: The Clash, Buzzcocks and The Jam.

The Jam, however, managed at the time by Paul Weller's father John, were uncomfortable with some of the core punk rituals and beliefs. As the tour progressed, inter-band friction began to increase, with Clash bassist Paul Simonon not holding back his opinions. The Jam had come from a different source than the punk big names, their base out of town, their music informed by the past – albeit the recent past – with their foreground instruments '60s Rickenbackers played with dexterity and style. Somehow, The Jam did not fit into this movement of punk's capital city heartland into the shires. They did not look punk. They did not sound punk. They were not punk. In due course, The Jam were no longer part of the White Riot Tour.

But for those who saw the tour after that departure, there were religious conversions aplenty. As with those who saw the Sex Pistols, watching The Slits, The Clash or Subway Sect could be both an affirmation and a reflection of working-class truth: that young people were bored, skint, ignored and frustrated. The members of these bands were not high and mighty deities like those in Led Zeppelin or Pink Floyd, trapped in the golden cages of their dressing rooms. These were musicians who would drink at the bar and have a chat. They were human-sized, for all that their music was epic, incendiary and inspirational.

Punk energy was intense and free-flowing, the music to the point, the bands young – as young as the audience, sometimes – and the musicians down to earth. This was a new beginning. This felt like a revolution. Hundreds of keen music fans were changed by this tour, as thousands were by seeing the Sex Pistols. A movement was spreading, its word the lore of The Clash, its signature voice Johnny Rotten, its look by Vivienne Westwood. This was real life, not some fantasy existence dreamed up by unapproachable rock stars. It was *relevant.* It was now.

Clash fan Hank Hansford recalled the band in their early prime.

I had told my parents I was staying at a mate's house, as I'm pretty sure they would not have let me go where I was going. We met at a local supermarket where the older ones amongst us bought several cans of Skol lager – then it was on the minibus to Bath Pavilion to see The Clash. When we arrived, the place was full of punks dressed in zips and chains, with a multitude of coloured mohicans and spiky hair colours. We went inside ready for the support act, who were supposed to have been The Slits, but unfortunately something had happened and they couldn't make it. I can't remember who replaced them, but it didn't really matter as we had come for The Clash anyway! Then the time arrived, and on they came on stage, starting off with 'Safe European Home' then thundering through numerous others thereafter, including such gems as 'Clash City Rockers,' 'White Man In Hammersmith Palais,' 'Tommy Gun,' and many others. I vividly remember the last two songs being 'Garageland' and 'White Riot.' I also remember plenty of flying beer glasses, not to mention all the gob as well. I can honestly say it was one of the best nights of my life. When it was all over, we went on the minibus back to my mate's house, and my parents were none the wiser.

The Clash went on to bigger things, though not necessarily better. Yet their message, their style, their authenticity and inspirational energy continued. School teacher Jon High also saw The Clash at one of their early gigs.

Dave Ratcliffe was my pal at school. We both went to St Mary's College in Blackburn, but with punk beginning to happen Dave's head was a bit turned by it. We were supposed to be a bit posh. We attended a 'nice' school. Punk was not a thing for us…

The Clash were a big deal for school lads.

Dave was captivated by the energy, the excitement, and the accessibility of punk rock. His favourite band was The Clash. He made me listen to their album for about two months before they appeared in Blackburn. This was a great night, opened by the support group Suicide. I remember the lead singer wiped the microphone across his cheek, which caused a deep bleed. This was the provocation the lads from Blackburn needed to launch a hail of gob – left, right and centre (with an occasional bottle thrown in) at this unfortunate performer. Hilarious at first, the shower was so unrelenting that I felt sad for the artist – and a little ill! The performance stopped short as the band requested the audience were a little more appreciative of the music, but the gob just continued to rain in. So they withdrew from the stage.

Then it was time for The Clash.

When the Clash came on, the gob relented. 'Drug Stabbin' Time,' 'Complete Control' and – for a town with ethnic issues – 'White Riot' were all to the fore. Absolutely brilliant, with no encore of course. Exhausted from 45 minutes of pogoing, I had just about had enough. As the lights came back on, the announcer exhorted us to buy tickets for the next performer in a week's time: "A great band from New York – Blondie." Dave and I had never heard of them. We weren't going to that.

While pogoing was a punk-appropriate dance that in the mosh pit made a lot of sense, gobbing at bands during gigs had more of an enigmatic origin. Most, if not all punk musicians loathed this sign of audience appreciation, but it continued nevertheless. When Siouxsie Sioux attempted to reason with her audience, telling them to stop spitting at her, they carried on, even when she walked off in protest. When Steve Jones tried to get the audience to stop unloading phlegm at him, they just ignored him. For that audience, gobbing at the Pistols *et al* was a kind of communion, forming a bond of class loyalty. Some people connect by shaking hands: punks connected via phlegm. Various explanations for gobbing have emerged over the years, sourced in the accidental deeds of Rat Scabies of The Damned, and in Johnny Rotten himself, but nobody really knows. An article written by John Black of the *Evening Standard* is also rumoured to have started the tradition. But some origin events are forever lost to history.

What is true is that the health consequences of gobbing could be serious. Joe Strummer acquired glandular fever from gob, while Siouxsie Sioux developed conjunctivitis. Perhaps it was a male rite, since no records of women delivering a phlegm volley have come down from those times.

I asked Eddie of The Vibrators for his memories of the phenomenon.

We hated that, and I tried to set the drums up as far back as possible to avoid it. Thankfully, if we told people to stop, they usually did. The first

> *time we came across it was when the Pistols played in Amsterdam with us, and their English fans gobbed at them. Thankfully it didn't last too long, as fans had a lot of respect for the bands.*

Lora Logic also encountered gobbing.

> *I never used to fret about what I was going to wear on stage, although with X-Ray Spex pretty much from the first gig I wore a full length plastic mac from Woolworths, which was a functional piece of fashion as the habit of Roxy punters was to spit – the gobbing era. The audience would gob at you quite aggressively. I never could make out whether this was praise, or because they felt it was a punky thing to do. Poly always felt it was quite disgusting, as did I, and the worst thing was I'd get quite a lot of spit down the bell of my saxophone – and who knows what kind of diseases I could have got from that. It didn't happen quite so much at other venues. It was quite repulsive.*

By the end of the 1970s, punk had mutated into New Wave amongst other genres, and the explosion was over, along with gobbing. But the post-punk environment proved to be fertile ground for one band in particular.

Chapter 21

Strangled

There never was a Guildford Strangler. Also, Guildford is not much of a rock 'n' roll sobriquet for a band trying to make it big on the pub circuit. So it made sense for this quartet to reduce it to The Stranglers. By the time they were beginning to attract attention under this name, the punk movement was at hand and everything was going back to basics, or, in some cases, even further. So for The Stranglers there was an immediate question. To jump on, or not to jump?

Although it was an article of punk faith that fancy instruments, synthesizers and songwriting chops were not part of the movement, much of that attitude came from the publicists of the time – the Malcolm McLarens of the world, for instance. Even some of the most recognisable characters had one foot in their favourite corner of Britain's musical past. To McLaren's annoyance, John Lydon referred in one interview to his liking for Magma and Van Der Graaf Generator. Captain Sensible meanwhile was a bit of a hippie at heart, a keen fan of jazz rock supremo John McLaughlin; and he liked psychedelia. Punk edges were blurred, punk influences multifarious.

Still, when a quartet of talented sorta-punks called The Stranglers appeared in town at the beginning of the punk explosion, they were rejected. Dave Greenfield looked like a prog muso who played his battery of keyboards suspiciously well. Moreover, there was a hint of The Doors to this band's sound, and that did not feel right. One of their songs, *Sometimes,* featured an instrumental section longer than eight bars. It was all a bit much for those hunting for that primeval punk vibe.

The Stranglers were also suspicious for other reasons. Older and more experienced on the circuit than your average punk, their drummer was ancient, a successful businessman with a fleet of ice cream vans, whose name was not Jet Black. This band did not seem like punks at all, their music too complex, their sound too musical. Yet they hung around. And they acquired fans.

From the perspective of the band itself, punk was something to align to. Like all bands hoping for success, they knew they had to follow every lead in their quest for fame and fortune; and punk was explosive enough to generate a ton of free publicity. When it came to choosing the opening song for their debut LP, *Sometimes* was the one. It did have a punk sound to it – a lead in, as Hugh Cornwell put it in a 2000 interview with Jim Drury, to music a little more intelligent afterwards. Thus, The Stranglers were simultaneously divorced from true punks, associated with it by the press, and in hock to its perceived mode of operation. Aggression was commonplace at their early gigs, with objects thrown at them by audiences. They kept going, always refining their sleazy sound.

They were a magical combination, a whole far greater than the sum of their remarkable parts. Chance is at once the great leveller of creative individuals (though they rarely know that) and also their route to glory. Their distinctive bassist Jean-Jacques Burnel – always called John by the inner circle – was originally a classical guitarist, before Cornwell, also a talented guitarist, convinced him to take up bass. As a consequence, many of Burnel's early bass parts exploited the further reaches of his instrument, as he constructed lines and runs as a guitarist might. Then there was the accident of the amp. Burnel, contrary to received wisdom, fed his bass into a guitar amp, which combined with his plectrum technique close to the bridge gave his sound extra twang and bite. When the amp cab began blowing speakers, that sound acquired a grit and thrum impossible otherwise to obtain. As record execs at the time told Cornwell, the fans loved that guttural bass sound. It instantly identified the band's unique music. Yet by the time they reached 1978 and their masterpiece *Black And White,* Burnel's amp cab was almost beyond repair, and after 1979 his sound was never replicated, though attempts were made.

Hugh Cornwell was a brilliant lyricist, using his life experiences (often involving women) and more surreal concerns to craft songs of great distinction. He sought the strange and the unusual in his guitar sound, although, akin to Robby Krieger of The Doors, he could still write a delightful guitar solo when he wanted to. His voice was flexible enough to create strange, almost animal-like utterances alongside tuneful performances. He could snarl with the best of them, yet his rich, smooth voice could also lilt and keen.

Jet Black's real name was Brian Duffy. In a band senior to the older punks, he was the oldest. He had built up a good business in the Surrey area, but drumming was his passion, at first in jazz. He was the rock of the band in the early days, when they were so skint they would eat nuts and raisins and drink Guiness as the best available balanced meal.

These three men could be dark. Very dark. The Stranglers acquired a kind of greasy, gothic aura as they refined their sound and developed their look and stagecraft through the middle of the seventies. Black was their colour. They received and doled out aggression, they baited the music press, they were perceived as being difficult or even dangerous. Yet at the hub of this intense, glossy darkness lay one of music's most gorgeous hearts.

Dave Greenfield was a prog rock lover brought into the band after a successful audition following the departure of Hans Warmling. A fan of Rick Wakeman and other caped luminaries, he transformed the sound of what would otherwise have been a traditional, if distinctive and intelligent, pub rock band. In due course he admitted that he did know a few Doors tracks, allowing the music press to harp on once again about the band not being proper punks. Moreover, he was in the same cachet as Wakeman and the rest of prog's synth gods, since his playing technique was of a very high order. This, however, was in part because of something never revealed during his lifetime, which was that he was a high functioning autistic.

Band members recall how discomfort or inappropriate behaviour marked him out in social situations as somehow "a bit different." He would take metaphorical or jocular references literally, leading conversations down various unexpected rabbit holes. His musical ability though was prodigious, his use of fluttering, hypnotic arpeggios piercing the centre of the band's black beauty. Once heard, that rippling Hohner Cembalet was impossible to forget. Indeed, few instrument sounds in rock have been so distinctive. Rather than improvise or let the music dictate what he might play, he would learn by heart lengthy keyboard parts, including all the variations and idiosyncrasies, before recordings. This often took a lot of time. By the time the band's breathless two album and umpteen gig 1977 was over and they faced a chill 1978, Greenfield was discovering a new generation of synthesizers, which in due course would make the third Stranglers album one of the all-time rock masterpieces. He was the mesmeric sun in the band's long night. His keyboards bubbled like refreshing spring water through shitty sewers. His synths brought colour to monochrome. When he died of complications brought about by Covid-19, many in the world of music mourned.

With the band acquiring an enthusiastic following, gigging regularly and accumulating a notable collection of songs, it was not long before they were noticed by record company scouts. They signed with United Artists and went to record at Fulham's T. W. Studios. In the cold, early months of 1977 they began working with two men vital to their first recordings, engineer Alan Winstanley and producer Martin Rushent. Recordings went well, and soon enough the master tapes were off to Olympic Studios in Barnes for mixing.

This debut album was in effect a studio freeze-frame of the best of their live set. The songs were melodic, striking, capturing all the unique elements of the band's sound, and they sounded like nothing else available at the time. Because the label wanted a single straight away, the band recorded Cornwell's song *Grip* and its soon-to-be B-side *London Lady* without delay, so that their debut 45 would be out before the album. *Grip* was the perfect single: unforgettable, striking, melodious. Martin Rushent, aiming for a wall of guitars, had Cornwell record the guitar parts over and over again, which in parallel with Greenfield's rippling keyboards gave the song fantastic momentum and energy. The lyrics referred to the band working for very little money and feeling like they were already imprisoned by the music biz. But they were excited about what was happening. *Grip* hit the charts at number 44 in its first week, and expectations were high for a top 20 placing the following week. There was plenty of airplay and the reviews were excellent. Yet the song vanished without trace.

Cornwell insists that chart compilers BRMB deliberately made the "mistake" which cost the band a smash hit. The Stranglers were, if not punks exactly, misfit outsiders with an aggressive attitude, and at the time that was more than enough to ensure dodgy dealings. Yet the record label, sensing that they were onto a winner with The Stranglers and keen to push for more, decided to release the controversial *Peaches* as a second single, reassuring the band that every effort would be made to ensure a hit and maximum publicity. The song, released in May of that year, peaked at number 8.

As for the album, it was clearly a classic. Everything about it was notable: the lurid cover, with Dave and Jean-Jacques at the front and a mysterious dark silhouette in the background, that unmistakeable sound, the lyrics, the vibe, the unusually long song at the end set into four movements. It sold well, becoming in due course one of the best-selling LPs of the time. Originally called *Dead On Arrival,* that title was changed at the last minute in a classic piece of Stranglers mayhem, adding enigma to their notoriety. *The Stranglers IV: Rattus Norvegicus* was lengthy, but it hit the mark. There was a lot to take in around this band, yet the campaign worked, with the *NME* placing it as their tenth best album of the year.

Keen to capitalise on this success, a second album went into production almost immediately. Some of the cuts were unused songs from the first batch of recordings, so when the band returned to T. W. Studios, and Winstanley and Rushent, there was a relationship and working method already set up. Through June and July they recorded the additional tracks which would augment a second, swift release in September. A new single came out with unseemly haste: *Something Better Change,* released in July, featuring a bravura vocal from Burnel: *Don'tcha like the way I seem to enjoy it? Stick my fingers right up your nose.* But the gem of the set was *No More Heroes,* yet another gorgeous earworm and a top ten hit, peaking at number 8. With the track bringing Burnel's bass and Greenfield's mesmeric keyboard arpeggios to the fore, and with some of Cornwell's best lyrics so far – witty, surreal, historical, intelligent – it was a tour de force.

Reviewers recognised that the band were capitalising on their reputation as punk's misogynists and press-baiters. There had been a vague sense of restraint on the debut album, a kind of sop to English manners, with some controversial themes and lyrics, and a glimpse of the band's sleazy, uneasy dark side. On the second LP however there was no holding back. *I Feel Like A Wog* was the opening cut, a sneering, sarcastic view of prejudice, followed by songs about suicide, sexism, and perverted school relationships. There was a bleak ferocity to the sleaze this time, supported by the no holds barred arrangements and vibe of aggression. It was the same, but nastier. The album received praise at the time, but already the band were pondering their place in the grand scheme of things. Lumped into the punk movement by the press, and keen to exploit whatever they could of the new explosion, they nevertheless sensed that they were different; set apart from the scene by virtue of age, background, keyboards and musicianship.

Does it matter whether or not The Stranglers were a punk band? In one sense, yes. In another sense, no.

That they were pilloried and rejected by the "real punks" is not in doubt. One notorious fight had members of The Clash with music journalists on their side lined up against the band and their fans. The aggression of their first clutch of songs and the virulence of the second batch made no difference to perceptions. Punks called them heretics, citing various reasons, then cast them into the wilderness. They were older than the punk norm, far more musical, had a synthesizer player, and could quote Ozymandias in one of their uglier songs. That they were not perceived as punks does matter, since the attitudes of the time, inside the movement and outside, are vital to its history. In a clash with the Sex Pistols, The Ramones and other spiky-haired notables, peacenik and all round good guy Dave Greenfield found himself shoving John Lydon against the side of a van behind Dingwalls. So as they toiled and worked the beer-stained clubs and venues of the south-east, a siege mentality grew, casting them as punk's outsiders and making them exaggerate their already provocative tendencies. In one such incident a music press journalist was gaffer taped upside down to the Eiffel Tower. Yet even these events, which Malcolm McLaren might have called Situationist, merely widened the abyss. Punk was becoming a movement of varied elements only months after its explosion onto the British media scene. Like all such movements, after the fuel was lit, the spark generated and the big bang created, what followed was largely a matter of chaos and semi-random elements. The Stranglers were one of those elements, labelled as punk, riding the wave, yet rejected by the hardcore inner circle of the movement.

That it does not matter is evinced by the naïve idealism of some early punk characters, before all the negative publicity and people like McLaren doing everything possible to exploit that publicity, fanning the waves of media shock and loathing, playing up to fears of anarchy and class war. As Dave Vanian explained in his *Guardian* interview, punk in the early days was as much about individualism as about a mob of anarchists running along London's greasy streets. The British establishment, alongside its cronies and apologists, have always reserved a particular scorn and callousness for those of the nation who, like a nail emerging from a plank of wood, stand out. In Britain, nobody is supposed to stand out, unless they have money and can label themselves a British Eccentric, in which case it is acceptable. Punk may have mutated into spiky dyed hair, safety pins and ripped clothes, but before that it was a cry for individualism, for acceptance of divergence from the norm, for a new adolescent identity set apart from deference and homogeneity.

The Stranglers were part of the need for a new individualism outside of establishment norms – and that included media norms. They did rebel like punks, and they did resort to aggression and violence like punks, and their music was filled with adult themes and gritty, disturbing lyrics, just like punk rock. They reserved so much of their venom for the mass media of the time, including a music press in hock to the punk crowd, because they felt ostracised. They should not have been ostracised. They had a right to join the movement and celebrate some of its founding principles. The echoes of events playing out as they laboured, and chased, and hung around covered them all: a cloud of opprobrium. But punk was about following a path regardless of the establishment's opinion. Perhaps Cornwell's sentiments in *I Feel Like A Wog – I feel like a wog, people giving me the eyes… I feel like a wog, I don't wanna go home… I feel like a wog, I don't mean you no harm* – applied to them, experiencing the sort of rejection felt by people of colour, by women, by gay people, and by others deemed worthy of contempt. Punk was a movement of opposition, of complaint, of emotional outburst. It was *worthy* of being noticed. The Stranglers, understanding that they were a great band, and with United Artists backing them, felt the same. They were *worth* taking note of.

Too often, the central tenets of a movement become written in stone, never to be deviated from. They become, in effect, the commandments of a religious faith, trotted out and adhered to regardless of reality – a reality that includes human beings. This applies to politics, to religion, and to much else in society. The central tenets of punk included being of humble origin, hating Pink Floyd, not having keyboards, not recording eight minute epics, and not being old. That the Stranglers were dark and virulent, that they baited journos and did women down mattered not one jot to most punks. The band were outsiders, and that was that.

Of course, this quartet of dark travellers had the last laugh. Yes, they were progressive, but that meant their music could *progress,* which was one of many reasons they outlasted almost every one of their peers, had a string of chart hits, lasted fifteen years with a stable line up, and even survived the departure of Hugh Cornwell. They remained true to Vanian's punk core belief, that the whole movement was about being allowed to do your own thing, winklepickers and goth make-up in his case, black leathers, the Hohner Cembalet and long instrumental solos for The Stranglers.

They were a punk manifestation, though they were not really punks. They had a punk attitude, though they were ostracised from the main movement. In the end, what mattered was that they were unique. 1977 was theirs for the taking, and when 1978 arrived a wide landscape lay at their feet. They moved on, nice and sleazy, filling the post-punk landscape with their enduring masterpiece.

Chapter 22

And Also...

The punk explosion did not happen only in London. Howard Trafford, soon to become Howard Devoto, and Peter McNeish, soon to be Pete Shelley, formed a band with a couple of other Bolton locals – an early version of Buzzcocks. Devoto's original plan had been to focus on electronic music, in 1975 a fast-changing genre led by the rise of German synthesizer titans Tangerine Dream, who had a couple of years earlier signed to Richard Branson's embryonic Virgin Records label, and who were recording a series of groundbreaking albums. Devoto was also a fan of other underground musical forms. The British punk explosion, however, changed everything. Having read a review of an early Sex Pistols gig, the Manchester duo headed south to watch the band play live – and they were both smitten. This was something full of excitement and sheer energy. By spring, Buzzcocks were playing live, and by summer the founding pair had prepared the way for what would be the momentous appearance of the Sex Pistols at Manchester's Lesser Free Trade Hall, a gig which would go down in legend amongst local soon-to-be musicians.

In July the band supported the Sex Pistols at another local gig, and soon they were opening for the Sex Pistols and The Clash in London, had appeared at the seminal 100 Club Punk Special, and had joined the Anarchy In The U.K. tour when The Damned fell away. Success was within their grasp.

Shelley and Devoto were nothing if not energetic. With the punk mantras *Do It Yourself* and *Do It Now* echoing around their minds, and with a number of quality songs already written, they decided to take matters into their own hands and release an EP. The music lacked the pop direction which would make the band – minus Devoto – nationally famous, but it was a huge and critical step on the way. *Spiral Scratch* was a bit rough and ready – laid down and mixed in a single day – but it was professionally recorded and produced, and released on their own independent New Hormones label in January 1977. They borrowed a large sum of money to finance the venture, but word of mouth and the excitement generated by the publicity stunts surrounding the Sex Pistols and other London bands meant that the run, one thousand discs, sold out. Mail order sales and support from local record shops also helped. Success was theirs.

I spoke with former Virgin Records MD Jon Webster about the *Spiral Scratch* EP. He found himself involved with it in an unexpected way.

> *I would sometimes sell tickets for big concerts, for instance at the Bingley Hall in Staffordshire. I'd run coaches to those gigs. There was good money there. Of course, I had to keep that separate from the Virgin money in case there were problems. When Spiral Scratch came out, Richard Boon, who managed Buzzcocks at the time, sold us about fifty copies. He signed a paper chit with the terms on it – that's how it was done at the time. The EP sold out really quickly at our shop, and I wanted more, but it had sold out everywhere. Richard told me the distributors weren't going to think about paying until thirty days had gone. So he had no money for a re-press. I asked how much he needed, then wrote him a cheque, on the condition that I got the first big chunk of the re-pressed batch. Howard Devoto wrote to me later, thanking me for my help.*

Devoto, however, soon saw that punk was not going to last much longer. He left the band because he felt the direction the movement was taking did not match his own instincts. He smelled something rotten in the increasingly frantic promotional events. He sensed individuality leaking out of the movement's pores. It was time for a new direction; in his case, the critically acclaimed post-punk group Magazine.

Pete Shelley, blessed with as much drive as Devoto and with pop songwriting chops, took on leadership of Buzzcocks, recruited a new bassist, and went on to write a number of classic punk and pop-punk chart hits. Having signed to the multinational UA record label, the band began work with Martin Rushent (producer for the first clutch of Stranglers albums) and were seen on tour with The Clash and playing *Top Of The Pops;* fame and fortune were theirs. But by the time Shelley had mastered his on-camera look and miming technique for the hits *Ever Fallen In Love* and *What Do I Get?* the punk explosion was over and everything had become New Wave.

Chelsea were one of the earliest punk bands to hit London. Assembled by the two owners of King's Road fashion emporium Acme Attractions, the band's name resonated in suitable style with the London borough they worked in. Steph Raynor and John Krivine were those individuals, and they placed Gene October (aka John O'Hara) and William Broad at the front of the band, with Tony James on bass and John Towe behind the drum kit. The latter two musicians had form – they had been in London SS. But after only a handful of gigs playing cover versions, the band fragmented, with Broad and James departing. A second version of the band became active as 1976 turned into 1977, with new musicians supporting Gene October, but even then the arriving/departing turnstile continued to rotate, with more leave-takings and yet more new arrivals. By summer, the band was stable enough to record a well-received punk single for Step Forward Records called *Right To Work,* a song which hit the mark enough to feature on the *Jubilee* soundtrack, a film in which Gene October acted. The band continued to record and gig for a couple of years, but as punk became something to look at in the rear view mirror, only October remained to keep the band alive. This, however, he did with some critical and commercial success.

James and Broad meanwhile were not sitting around moaning about bad times (internal friction in Chelsea had been excessive, with October considering Broad and James too enamoured with rock fame and fortune, and the commercial music which went with that lifestyle). Broad, though, had by now changed his name to something with much more panache, a name with which he would in due course become famous: Billy Idol. Idol had excellent punk connections, being an associate of the Bromley Contingent, and, to further improve his reputation, dropping out of uni to play more guitar and get into the punk scene. When the heat inside Chelsea became too intense, he, James and Towe departed to form Generation X. This band was for a while managed by Andrew Czezowski, no longer working with The Damned, and associated with Acme Attractions by reason of being their accountant.

Idol in particular was keen to present himself as a star in waiting. He had a high opinion of himself and looked great in front of a camera. How could Generation X fail? All he had to do was give up playing guitar to become a singing legend.

Soon gigging began in earnest, including one at the just-opened Roxy Club, run by Czezowski and Susan Carrington, an event which also featured Siouxsie and the Banshees. Once cover versions of older material had been abandoned, the band was set to shine. But Czezowski turned out to be more interested in managing the Roxy, already going from strength to strength, and so new management was put in place: journalist Jonh Ingham and Stewart Joseph of Rough Trade, which by then was a record company as well as a shop. As 1977 began to warm up and turn into the Year Of Punk, the band gigged wherever they could and began a recording schedule designed to get them noticed. But with further friction coming from the increasingly commercial direction created by Idol and James, there followed a new drummer, international dates, and a somewhat ambiguous relationship with musicality that was at odds with their image. Idol was not immune to criticism, something which irked his otherwise idolised self. Soon the band began to open themselves up to criticisms of not being punk enough, being too interested in popularity and success, and paying too much attention to how they looked: middle class wannabes, as some had it. But the core duo of Idol and James ploughed on, creating their own direction, taking the flak, until they began to get what they wanted. Success.

By autumn, that tactic paid off. They were playing on *Top Of The Pops,* and there was no higher calling than that.

Generation X continued riffing on punk and what it stood for, but they were now being spoken of more in terms of commercial success and pop viability than for the quality of their lyrics or the authenticity of their attitude. Idol was keen to be seen. James wrote most of the lyrics, few of which now dealt with working-class issues. The music press began to label their sound as empty, their lyrics banal rhetoric, and the band itself as gatecrashers on the punk movement. By 1979 the writing was on the wall, with the band forced to discuss the comparative lack of commercial success with their record label.

Yet they did have their fans, and many were enthusiastic. Generation X fan Neal Vaughan spoke about his memories of the band in their early days.

After skiving off a Friday from school, we were on a train taking us to Bournemouth for a Generation X gig. On our arrival we sussed out where the village bowl was and were rewarded by a glimpse of the band, the unmistakable peroxide hair of Billy disappearing into the venue. Next, we sorted a B&B, as we couldn't get home that evening. £8 paid for the two of us. We talked to two other punks staying there who had come down from London for the gig.

At the venue we walked into a packed bar – safety pins and spikey haired people everywhere (not the London postcard punks). Pints were bought and we happily listen to the punky disco. We were informed that the first band were going on stage. We thought it was great having three bands.to see. We moved into what look like an underground football terrace sloping down to the stage. The Straightjackets were on first – fast and basic music – then The Jolt, who were more musically accomplished. Both bands were greeted by lots of gobbing. But when Generation X took the stage it looked like it was raining. We started the gig about four rows down from the stage, but ended up near the back due to frenzied pogoing and me being a smallish sixteen year old. The set went on: 'Wild Youth,' 'Day By Day,' '100 Punks,' a slight rest with 'Kiss Me Deadly,' then back to 100 mph 'Youth Youth Youth.' We were absolutely sweating buckets by this stage, but I was caught up in the rebellion-fuelled atmosphere of my first gig. All too soon the gig was over, with encore 'My Generation' being the last song. The music was over but my ears rang for the next twenty-four hours.

The next morning we went for breakfast in a café, and they had a poster advertising the gig. I've still got it 46 years later.

Sham 69 formed in, of all places, leafy and sophisticated Surrey, taking the first part of their name from the last syllable of the town of Hersham. Like so many of the original English punk bands, their music and direction was transformed when they attended a Sex Pistols gig. From then on, much changed. Their charismatic and intense front man was Jimmy Pursey, who like Pete Shelley would adopt an unforgettable stage persona for the band's many *Top Of The Pops* appearances. 1976 was spent changing membership and honing their songs, with only Pursey remaining, but by 1977 the band in their most recognisable form were ready to break out of the loaded commuter belt that had birthed them. Their debut 45 was released on the small Step Forwards record label in summer 1977, produced by none other than John Cale of Velvet Underground, and its small-scale success got them signed to Polydor Records. By the time of their string of chart hits however the punk movement had blown itself out, leaving the band to struggle with gig violence, unwanted political dalliances from various fan sectors, and, in 1979, their departure from the live circuit following a National Front incident in London.

Pursey soon became disillusioned with the financial imperatives of the music business, and went on to pilot a number of commercially unsuccessful projects, including one with ex-Sex Pistols Cook and Jones. Sham 69, however, had marked the British music scene with their unique sound and attitude.

Eater, one of the lesser-known bands from the initial punk explosion, were in fact one of the more remarkable ones. When they started out they were at school in their home district of Finchley, all of them between the ages of fourteen and seventeen. In 1976, these four lads, Ashruf and Lutfi Radwan, aka Andy Blade and Social Demise, Brian Haddock, aka Brian Chevette, and Ian Woodcock formed the band, with the intention of making high intensity punk music. Their debut performance in Manchester preceded the first Damned and Sex Pistols singles, the gig featuring none other than Buzzcocks as their support. By the end of the year they were gigging in London on the nascent punk circuit, and as 1977 began they scored two appearances at the Roxy Club, one of them with The Damned as support. Other punk notables associated with their trailblazing gigs were Sham 69 and The Lurkers. Soon, gigs at the Roxy were coming every month. For school kids in the middle of the seventies, this was quite an achievement.

Soon there was talk of recording deals, 45s and even an LP. One of the producers of the time, Dave Goodman, best known in punk circles for his work with the Sex Pistols, was taken on to work with the youthful band, who had signed with local indie label The Label. Goodman was another remarkable character of the era, who after his early punk work became a full-on hippy, part of the rainbow collective New Age Radio, channeler of aliens, and one of the movers behind Mandala Records, with whom New Age Radio were associated. Goodman produced a clutch of three singles for the band: *Outside View*, *Thinking Of The U.S.A.*, and *Lock It Up*. Released over six months in 1977, these cuts were fast, raw and powerful. During this period they also gave two tracks to the Roxy Club's compilation album, and even appeared in Don Letts' classic montage film *The Punk Rock Movie.*

The LP appeared at the end of the year, again produced by Goodman. *The Album* featured original material and a few high intensity covers. Though the relative youth of the band was noted, their enthusiasm and achievements were also recognised at the time by reviewers, although some were not too impressed. Mark Perry of *Sniffin' Glue* memorably wrote them off as lacking any musical ideas, while John Savage remarked that their youth by itself was not enough. By 1978 the band were beginning to fragment and fade, with Chevette departing. A live EP was their swansong, released by the faithful The Label. The band parted company with one another in 1979, Woodcock going on to play with The Vibrators.

The Maniacs were another first generation punk band from 1976. Finding themselves a trio with guitarist and vocalist Alan Lee Shaw at the helm, their debut outing in this format was at the Mont De Marsan First International Punk Festival. A second guitarist thickened the live sound, but changes later on left them as a three piece again. The well-received debut single *Chelsea 1977* backed with *Ain't No Legend* converted more fans, while a couple of tracks, *I Ain't Gonna Be History* and the catchy *You Don't Break My Heart* augmented the *Live At The Vortex* LP – another success. The band, now managed by *Sounds* music press photographer Ian Dickson, got a deal with U.A., their five track demo produced by Dave Goodman.

Alan Lee Shaw recalled Goodman and the recording session at Pathway Studios.

The Maniacs recorded 'Chelsea 77' at Pathway Studios in London on 09/10/1977. Dave Goodman was a decent guy, somewhat maligned, and certainly unsung in the annals of punk. Dave's talent lay in the fact that he gave over his time and talent to the shambles that the early Pistols were, giving them and their music some kind of form and direction, and paving the way for Chris Thomas to finally give them the explosive production that the world now all knows and loves! Dave's influences came from the hippy-dippy days of the 1960s, and like a lot of like-minded others he hitched his wagon onto the burgeoning punk movement. He kindly produced our demos for our single 'Chelsea 77' on UA records. R.I.P. Dave.

I asked about those amazing times with The Maniacs in the seventies.

Being at the build-up and ultimate epicentre of the punk rock explosion in London '76/'77 was truly mind-blowing, with the new generation of snotty-nosed oinks attempting to rattle the cages of the UK's grey old establishment (we're talking mainly Pistols and Clash here), the foundations of which were ever so slightly rocking, albeit briefly. Nevertheless, we all felt part of what was on offer, and all too happy to ride it in spades; which we did, something I would not have missed for the world, and didn't! Through punk and forming my bands The Rings and The Maniacs, I finally felt I had a voice. The D.I.Y. nature of punk was totally liberating – we were free from conforming to big business, at least for a while. Punk rock's D.I.Y. attitude and legacy continues on through social media and the internet.

Gigs were close up, loud, ragged and in your face; there were no massive impersonal arena shows the like of which are so commonplace now.

I also asked about the craze for gobbing, which The Maniacs encountered.

The "spit show fracas" was horrid, childish, unnecessary, and thankfully short-lived. Sadly, punk rock now lives on mainly in a few ageing nostalgia acts, but I can say that being part of punk rock's first wave one had to be there to really feel its raw, visceral impact.

But 1977 saw the end of the road for this band, with Alan Lee Shaw moving on to The Physicals. The Maniacs split early in 1978.

Subway Sect were another of the bands at the 100 Club Punk Special. Formed around their main man Vic Godard, various line-up changes occurred before they began recording under the stewardship of their manager Bernie Rhodes, whose more famous clients were The Clash. Early releases did not hit the charts, but the band toured alongside The Clash on numerous occasions, impressed Joe Strummer, and achieved that punk high water mark of a John Peel session.

Their luck did not remain good. Having managed to lay down tracks in preparation for the debut album, Rhodes washed his hands of the band in circumstances that remain murky to this day, with only Godard remaining on his books. Minor success in music paper circles during 1978 did little to help this situation. Godard reappeared some years later as a solo artist.

Meanwhile, far to the north, a remarkable punk band called Penetration were making their mark. Fronted by Pauline Murray, the band played various gigs during 1977, including support slots for Generation X, Buzzcocks, The Vibrators and The Stranglers. Murray had been energised into action following a Sex Pistols gig, and began following that band to the extent that she and her friends were known as the "Durham Contingent" in affectionate homage to Siouxsie Sioux's crowd. In May, the band played alongside an unknown group called Warsaw, who would go on to rename themselves Joy Division. The band soon recorded a pair of much-admired John Peel sessions and released singles and an album, also admired, but commercial success eluded them, although critical success, especially in the music press, was always theirs.

Another band appearing at the end of the punk years was The Ruts. Formed halfway through 1977, their arrival was catalysed by band members watching the Pistols onstage and by an inspirational Ramones T shirt. After various line-up changes, they began to evolve into a dub-influenced unit, but success never quite arrived, although John Peel was a vocal fan of them and their music. They played at various Rock Against Racism benefit gigs. In later years they supported The Damned, but the loss of Malcolm Owen following a heroin overdose marked the end of the original band (later they would re-emerge as Ruts DC). They are still admired for the Peel-endorsed debut single *In A Rut,* which remains a punk classic.

Stiff Little Fingers from Northern Ireland were another quartet of punkish lads inspired by the Sex Pistols, but their star shone brighter. A band playing classic rock covers that formed at school, they turned to punk soon after the movement broke out. The dire and dangerous political situation of the time inspired many of their best songs, and they were trailblazers in their country, with their debut album, in association with Rough Trade, becoming the first top 20 independent album. Their own label, Rigid Digits, was home to the first Northern Irish punk single, the classic cut *Suspect Device,* whose cover was unambiguous – an image of the kind of weapons being used by the Provisional IRA. Unsurprisingly, John Peel was an instant convert, becoming an enthusiastic supporter of both the 45 and band. When Geoff Travis of Rough Trade heard Peel play that momentous song he became another influential fan, a state of affairs leading to the band's distribution deal nationwide. By 1978, the band were well on course to stardom, though punk had by then changed into post-punk. In 1979, their debut LP *Inflammable Material* emerged – another instant classic.

One of the more unusual characters of the punk years was the "punk poet" John Cooper Clarke. A native of Salford (he also assumed the appellation Bard of Salford), his immediately recognisable voice, unusual genre and cult following propelled him into the limelight, whereupon his distinctive, Dylanesque appearance assisted in bringing fame and plaudits. Cooper Clarke was the epitome of that individualism lauded by The Damned's Dave Vanian. Inspired to write poetry while at school, he rode the punk wave with skill and prosodic grace. With a day job as a laboratory technician to keep himself financially afloat, he began performing at various clubs in Manchester, but that life was not easy. Minor success with a tiny record label, Rabid, and an EP and then an LP release all convinced him that there was a possibility of making it as punk's poet-in-residence. Family support helped. By the time punk blew itself out and mutated into New Wave, he was becoming established nationally, with tours, sessions and further releases on Beggars Banquet and CBS Records all arriving in due course. He performed alongside major punk bands, including the Sex Pistols, Siouxsie and the Banshees and Buzzcocks, not to mention Joy Division in later years. A solitary presence on stage, his mode of delivery, accent and striking appearance all made him a beloved figure of the era, a position cemented by a classic John Peel session recorded in 1978 which included his poems *Health Fanatic* and *I Married A Monster From Outer Space.*

Teacher Jon High saw John Cooper Clarke in the poet's early days, recalling that evening well.

> *Dave Ratcliffe and I managed to blag a lift to Preston Guild Hall to see an artiste who at the time I thought was the most exciting in the world –*

Elvis Costello. He was about to release the 'Armed Forces' LP. At the gig, he played 'Oliver's Army,' which was due to be released in two weeks.

There were two supports – but we weren't bothered about them. Richard Hell and the Voidoids received the usual abuse and Lancastrian booing. And then… a scruffy, scrawny, Mancunian sounding bloke turned up to feed us poetry! He was absolutely brilliant. He held the venue completely. At this gig I heard 'Beesley Street' for the first time. A genius. How did this poet fit in with a high energy semi-punk night? But he did.

Our confusion was displaced after Elvis turned up and regaled us with hits – and material that was shortly to become hits. But it was John Cooper Clarke who was the highlight of the evening.

What was it like though if you were not John Lydon, Joe Strummer or Rat Scabies? What about the innumerable bands formed in the white heat of the explosion who never got lucky, never had enough cash to press their own vinyl on their own label, or who were riven by internal dissent? There were too many to count. The majority are unknown to punk history.

I spoke to retired nuclear environmental safety officer Kenneth O'Brien about his experiences of the movement to discover what it was like if you did not succeed or get famous via the punk revolution.

The first indication I had that something was about to happen was when I read a small piece in one of the music magazines (I can't remember which one, but probably either Sounds or NME). The news item related to some trouble at a London gig involving a band called the Sex Pistols. It was a few weeks later that things began to happen. The Pistols were being mentioned more and more in the music press and was gaining some notoriety. I was curious, but not enthralled. My music tastes at the time ran from Rainbow (local boy Jimmy Bain was playing bass at the time), Peter Frampton, SAHB, and a whole host of others. Little did I know back then that soon some of my friends would begin calling me a boring old fart (I was fifteen).

It transpired that, like so many musicians of the time, the Sex Pistols were the catalyst.

We had a small, local record shop. It's long gone now, but I still see Jean, the owner at the time. Nice lady who was always willing to try and get what her customers asked for. I asked if she could get me a copy of the newly released 'Anarchy In The U.K.' It wasn't bad. Almost verging on heavy rock, I thought. I listened to it a couple of times but then gave it to a schoolmate who was much more interested in it than I was. More on that school mate later. Imagine! I had an original EMI copy of Anarchy and I just gave it away! What would that be worth today, I wonder. That was it for me. My first toe dip into the world of punk rock but the water was far too cold. I preferred to cosy up with my warm rhythm and blues.

Kenneth and his school friend Vic began to feel the nation's vibes changing.

The social and musical dividing lines began to come down. Punks hung out with punks, heavy metal fans etc hung out with their own. There was no violence between the factions that I recall, and this was probably because everybody knew each other. There was, however, an explosion of bands. Punk had proved to all (myself included) that you didn't have to be Ritchie Blackmore to write a decent song. I had only just started to teach myself guitar the year before so, even though punk music itself didn't enthral me, the whole philosophy of (as we say in Scotland) just pick up a guitar and "gie it laldy" was a massive piece of inspiration and encouragement that I still embrace to this day.

And then, the inevitable formation of a band.

The school pal that I gave 'Anarchy In The U.K.' to had formed a band. It was called Some Action. He'd just fallen out with the guitar player, and he was looking for a replacement. Despite only knowing the most rudimentary chords (which turned out to be on a par with the previous member) I got the gig. I liked the way the band was headed. Other bands were writing songs about working in a factory and stuff like that. These were school kids, just like me. They had no idea what it was like to work in a factory. Peter, the singer and leader of Some Action, wrote songs about anger, frustration, lack of a future. I liked where his head was at so, despite wearing jeans, cowboy boots, sporting very long hair and playing a cheap copy of a Gibson Flying V, I became the guitarist for Some Action. It gave me my first taste of creativity as I strived to put music to Peter's words. I remember a couple of songs we wrote: 'Guns On The East Beach' (East Beach being one next to the town harbour). It was about having no hope and things angrily spiralling out of control.

Alas, the band was not destined for the big time.

We were playing with a number of other punk bands at the Victoria Ballroom. The venue has long been demolished, but this was a really big deal. Bands like the Bay City Rollers, The Corries and The Alexander Brothers had played there. Not only that, we were being filmed by some students from Edinburgh University. This was massive. Callum (the bass player) and I waited patiently for our slot. We spent most of our time wondering where Pete and Steve our drummer were. They rolled in just seconds before we were about to start. Callum and I were already on stage waiting, and it wasn't until Pete stood next to me that I realised both he and Steve were drunk as skunks. The gig was an absolute shambles. A complete disaster. At the end of our "performance" I said to Pete that I was leaving, and he threatened to kick the shit out of me. I decided to exit the venue when he was too pissed to attempt anything. To be fair, I bumped into him a couple days later and he apologised both for ruining the gig and for threatening violence. He didn't ask about the possibility of trying to salvage the situation and I didn't offer any hope. I think we both knew things had gone too far. It was a shame, because I think Pete wanted Some Action to be our town's version of The Damned and, to be honest, I'd have been quite happy if that had been the situation instead of the inebriated reality that it truly was.

Kenneth witnessed the end of the movement too.

There were a number of punk bands in town by this time, but most weren't doing very much. One stood out. It was called Wasted State and, again, I was friendly with the band members. They were building a bit of a fan following in the town and had achieved the ultimate in credibility – getting gigs in other towns. One infamous night, a bus was organised to take a load of us around thirty miles to another town to support Wasted State. It was a mixture of punks and others, and I was among the "others." It wasn't long after getting inside the venue that we sensed an air of hostility. It wasn't helped by the fact that some of us were giggling and ridiculing the "yokels" for looking like they'd just stepped out of 1974. Punk obviously hadn't reached this part of the sticks yet. Wasted State began their set. I thought they were putting on a good display, but they weren't going down well with the locals. After a bit of jeering and catcalling, the singer started answering back. That just made things worse. Wasted State began another of their songs, and then, out of nowhere, the singer moved to the edge of the stage and booted this particularly loud-mouthed local right in the face. All hell broke loose and I, being the coward that I am, made a hasty retreat back to the waiting bus in the car park. I was soon followed by quite a few others. The police arrived and things started to calm down, but we were told to leave town without delay. We even had a police escort for part of the way home. This unsavoury incident hit our local paper, and I think the punks revelled a little in their notoriety for a while. I was just glad to get out unscathed. That night was the only violence I witnessed during the birth of punk in my small town, and it was fuelled as much (I think) by traditional town rivalry as by any musical differences. The punk I knew in my town didn't really have any of this violent undercurrent towards other music lovers, and it wasn't unusual to see punks mixing with heavy metal fans and others. I think the common bond was our love of music. It really didn't matter what type of music you loved, it just mattered that you did. That was the high-water mark for punk in our little town. It still stumbled on for a few years after, but it had lost its initial shock value, and soon the differences between supporters of different genres started to melt away. This was helped by the emergence of Motorhead, who proved that punks and heavy metal fans could actually enjoy the same band. The first time I went to see them, I was surprised at how many punks were there but, the more I went, the more I saw it as the norm.

Kenneth concluded his recollection by explaining that safety pins and brightly coloured spiked hair did not actually last very long, and that rural punks morphed into "untidy dressers in black." It was now around the end of 1977 or early 1978, and local punks had made many trips into Edinburgh to see various bands; they had made some out-of-town friends. These city dwellers, he said, "would often come down to our little town for the weekend, and it was immediately apparent that in the city all the coloured spiked hair and safety pins was still hard core."

As Kenneth put it: "Undiluted punk was still alive and well in Auld Reekie."

Chapter 23

Don Letts, The Punk Rock Movie, & Film

Don Letts was a Londoner whose involvement in the punk movement covered music, film and DJ work. The son of Jamaican parents, he was much taken with dub and reggae music, to the extent that one summer's day just before punk took root via the Pistols, he blagged his way into Bob Marley's hotel and spoke to him. But it was with The Clash that Letts found himself most involved in punk circles. That band, plus the Sex Pistols, alongside other names such as Debbie Harry and Patti Smith, were all to be seen at Acme Attractions, the clothes shop he helped run on the King's Road. But that shop was far more than just a retailer of clothes; it was, like McLaren and Westwood's SEX, a punk haunt, a nexus of the new thinking, and a place for bands and musicians to hang out.

It was Letts amongst others who brought dub reggae in particular to London, inspiring many bands, not least The Clash. By now he was doing well out of DJing and the retail side of operations, so he changed tack, becoming (briefly) The Slits' manager, and shooting material for the film which would the following year become *The Punk Rock Movie.*

Letts began filming from his early days with punk bands. He owned a Super 8 film camera, which he used to capture band performances, as when he accompanied the White Riot Tour with The Clash. All of this was hand-held footage. But Letts was also to be seen – and often – at Andrew Czezowski and Susan Carrington's Roxy Club, where most of the core punk bands cut their teeth. He was a DJ there, mingling with the crowd, getting known, contributing to the movement. During the "100 Days of Punk" which are often said to characterise the Roxy in its heyday, he filmed many bands, including some destined to achieve great things. As word got around that he was filming, it was assumed that something of substance would emerge. This turned out in due course to be *The Punk Rock Movie.*

By the latter half of 1977 Letts had accumulated enough material to edit a collage of extraordinary punk live performances, all of them at the Roxy Club except the Sex Pistols, whom he filmed at Sid Vicious' first public gig with the band at the Screen On The Green. There were songs from The Clash, Sex Pistols, X-Ray Spex, Siouxsie and the Banshees, Johnny Thunder and the Heartbreakers, Eater, Wayne County and the Electric Chairs, Subway Sect, The Slits, Generation X and Slaughter and the Dogs. Interspersed between these performances were candid snippets of band members and their associates joking around, rehearsing and chatting. The film opened and closed with the Sex Pistols, songs including *God Save The Queen*, *Pretty Vacant* and *Liar.* The X-Ray Spex song was their classic *Oh Bondage!* Clash cuts included *White Riot* and *Garageland.*

The hour-long first edit of the film received a premiere showing in autumn 1977 at the ICA. Enough publicity was garnered from the film and from the media fuss surrounding the movement to bring a theatrical release, and also for the final cut of the film to make it to video. Both of these were released in 1978.

The film received a lot of credit at the time for its cinema verité qualities, accentuated by Letts holding the camera in hand as he shot. To this day it remains a remarkable document of those incendiary times.

There was one other notable punk film made during the 1970s. *Jubilee* was created in 1977 by Derek Jarman and Christopher Hobbs, with Jarman directing. Many punks of the time, such as Jordan and Wayne County, and a few post-punks in the making, including Adam Ant and Toyah Wilcox, appeared in it. Music was provided by Chelsea, Siouxsie Sioux and Steve Severin, who appeared on film as themselves, and Wayne County. Brian Eno was another notable musician involved with the project. Another punk of the time, Gene October, vocalist with Chelsea, played the character Happy Days, destined to come to a breathless end in red plastic.

Filmed in the silver jubilee year of 1977, the film told the tale of Queen Elizabeth I time-travelling into a ruined, dystopian England, there to observe the social decay of the nation and philosophise about it. With our 1977 monarch no longer at the top of the pyramid, the scene was set for various acolytes of meaningless violence and surreal set pieces to wander around the capital city, variously declaiming, fighting and breaking and entering before deciding to decamp to the Dorset countryside. The film's style and reason for existing owed much to punk. Without traditional sequential narrative and a three act structure, it rambled from scene to scene glorying in its grainy footage, much of which was shot in bomb-damaged districts of London, emphasising grim living conditions, ruin and squalor, and the kind of characters who too often have to live in such circumstances. These characters had suitably evocative names: Amyl Nitrate, Mad, Lounge Lizard and Chaos.

The film, which should perhaps have pleased the publicity-chasing punk cognoscenti of the day, was in fact criticised on various accounts. Vivienne Westwood designed and sold a T shirt which took Jarman to task for his "misrepresentation" of punk. Yet the film epitomised, and even celebrated both what punk was angry about and how it delivered its anger. The unforgettable scenes of blitz-ruined London, still to complete its resurrection thirty years after the end of World War 2, contrasted with uncomfortable intensity against the concluding scenes of bucolic West Country landscapes. This was a raw film, visceral like so much of the early punk sound. It lacked traditional structure, offering something novel, something more appropriate to a new, youthful generation. It followed its emotions and desires with impulsive speed; an almost indecent haste, in fact, albeit handled with panache by Jarman. Above all, in its depiction of social deprivation, political stalemate and bog-standard British toadying to royalty, it was a fusillade against established norms. It tried to speak truth to privileged power in the authentic voice of London's inner circle of punk, all the time knowing that the pillars of that power would not crumble. But at the same time it did offer punks and all who admired them a new cultural expression. In the time of *Star Wars* and *The Spy Who Loved Me,* it was a breath of fresh air. Like punk music itself, it was both an expression and an inspiration. It was intended to fulfil deviant dreams and discomfort the viewer; a riot on celluloid. In that regard, it succeeded.

Chapter 24

Ever Get The Feeling You've Been Cheated?

The final Sex Pistols tour was a jaunt across the redneck belt of America. It marked the demise of the band. As Lennon had put it eight years earlier, the dream was over.

Malcolm McLaren could have booked the Pistols into happening venues in New York or Boston, but audiences there might have perceived the band to be situationists, merry pranksters, or just as those people from England everybody was talking about. That was not what he wanted. With the Sex Pistols he had developed a managerial style based on causing the greatest amount of newsworthy chaos, a strategy designed to maximise both sales and attention. If New York audiences (which Lydon characterised as too pretentious to take seriously) began analysing their situationist street cred, that was not going to help shift LPs. What McLaren wanted was a tour of bunfights. He wanted front page splashes.

There were nine dates over twelve days taking in such cities as Dallas, Tulsa, Atlanta and Memphis. Warner Brothers put up a million dollar bond so that the band could get their two-week visas. Two of the dates were cancelled after the relevant authorities got cold feet, leaving a raucous, chaotic seven, concluding at the Winterland Ballroom in San Francisco.

The band was not in the best of health. Lydon was finding the pressure of being the press' whipping boy distressing, for all that he retained his confrontational attitude. His life with the band was turning into a war of attrition. Steve Jones and Paul Cook just wanted to play music. Sid Vicious was in the poorest shape, a lumpen amateur on his instrument at the best of times, now addicted to heroin and fading fast. It did not bode well.

As the band progressed towards their last ever date, some of the gigs turned out good, some not so well. With Vicious baiting audiences in his most unsubtle manner, plenty of food, beer cans and miscellaneous items were lobbed their way. One report describes Lydon receiving a pie full in the face – surely the perfect metaphor for what was happening. Lydon himself gave good vocal performances, but he was struggling beneath the weight of audience dislike. For two years the Sex Pistols had positioned themselves as the band everyone loved to hate, and that brought them record deals, notoriety, success of a sort. Yet not even the most confrontational of individuals can fight forever. Eventually, attrition takes its toll, physically and mentally.

Voyeuristic press leering in Atlanta meant that more hacks turned up for the gig there than fans of the band; and there were plenty of fire marshals in case of trouble. But according to audience recollections afterwards, the music itself was pretty good. In Memphis the following day the gig was oversold, meaning a couple of hundred fans were left to suffer the cold weather outside. Various underhand ploys sorted some of them out, but the gig itself turned into a band versus audience slog. In San Antonio two days later well over a thousand people turned up – a minority of them actual punks – and before long the gig descended into chaos. Sid Vicious crowned the evening with one of his most notorious comments at local characters, whereupon the bunfight McLaren desired began in earnest. Too loud and too ramshackle, the music was forgotten in this struggle between opponents. At Baton Rouge as many of the audience were looking for a fight as were looking to hear the band. In Dallas the next day Vicious carried on his ploy of taunting the audience, causing more trouble for everybody. In Tulsa the following day the atmosphere was more restrained, the venue only half full, the crowd a mix of curious locals and onlookers.

The final gig was on 14 January 1978 at Bill Graham's legendary Winterland Ballroom venue in San Francisco. By now, Lydon's voice was beginning to suffer, and fractious relationships between band members were coming to the boil. Steve Jones was suffering from a bad cold and Vicious was hardly bothering to play his bass on stage. McLaren meanwhile continued to follow his scorched earth management policy, encouraging trouble, or at least setting out the conditions for it to begin. It was now that a previously unmentionable concept, that of carrying on the band without McLaren at the helm, began to surface. Lydon in particular felt like an extension of McLaren's management style, a puppet of the puppet-master, there to do his whim and take all the resulting flak off the audience. It was obvious to him that McLaren had booked the tour to maximise negative publicity, encouraging a media shit-show spectacle. Local newspapers talked about how punk rock destroyed lives and how it would ruin the children of America. Lydon was beginning to see the end of the line.

The gig was supported by two local bands, The Nuns and The Avengers. The Pistols staggered onto the stage after them, Lydon in full sarcasm mode as he mocked the audience: "Welcome to London." The gig was broadcast live by the local KSAN-FM radio, with the broadcasters of the time almost too shocked to do their job: "I don't believe this is really happening, folks," one drawled in amazement. Again Lydon gave a good vocal performance under the circumstances, but he was struggling, and the rest of the band were little better. They played all their classic songs, opening with *God Save The Queen*, and including *Seventeen, EMI, Bodies, Holidays In The Sun* and *Pretty Vacant.* They concluded with *Anarchy In The U.K.*, before returning for an encore, The Stooges' *No Fun.* This lyric seemed to match something in Lydon's increasingly isolated, desolate mood, as the mantra *This is no fun, no fun, this is no fun at all...* echoed around the arena. He felt now that he was participating in a travesty of something which had once felt real, and into which he had poured all his feelings and thoughts. But this gig was more like slapstick for the amusement of crowing locals. This was absurd, and not in the Absurdist sense. It was gross, inauthentic and painful.

As he knelt in front of Cook's drum kit all these feelings manifested themselves in one of the most famous closing lines in music history: *Ha ha, ever get the feeling you've been cheated?* Then a final: *Goodnight.* He followed Vicious offstage.

There was worse to come. Following the Winterland Ballroom show, McLaren informed Lydon and the rest of the band that their next project involved working with Great Train Robber Ronnie Biggs, a resident in Rio de Janeiro in Brazil. For Lydon, this was the final straw. The idea was beyond absurd. To him it felt almost calculated to destroy. He realised that all those feelings which had welled up into his final audience taunt were genuine. The Sex Pistols were over, at least, with him as front man. He was out.

Cook and Jones however remained loyal to their impresario manager, travelling with him to Rio de Janeiro, where they all got stuck into enjoying various local entertainments. Sid Vicious meanwhile was en route to a New York hospital. Lydon now felt isolated as never before, betrayed and disillusioned. He gathered all his resources, accumulating enough cash to buy a one way ticket to New York, where he announced that the Sex Pistols had split up.

The chaotic two year sprint was over.

The band overturned innumerable sacred cows, recorded an LP deemed forever a classic, and aimed enough barbs at the British establishment for some to live on through history. But above all they helped smash apart music business operations to the extent of fostering an entirely new subculture, independent music on independent labels – indie music as it would be known. That subculture would soon become a culture; a new musical environment. The band inspired more musicians and groups than any other in British music history, with the exception perhaps of The Beatles, to whom they were akin in the sense that they blazed new trails through hidebound British culture. And they undertook this devastating, extraordinary sprint in a way impossible to imagine years later, when their legacy became the norm. There was BP and there was AP: Before Pistols and After Pistols. They were the bridge across that divide, the vehicle and the message too. They were the real deal.

Chapter 25

Diversification & Death

The diversification of punk was not long in arriving.

One of the most significant of the first wave of punk bands was Wire. A quintet formed in London just before punk began to hit mainstream media, they played at the Roxy Club on 19 January 1977 and appeared on the era-defining *The Roxy London WC2* live album. Colin Newman, vocalist and guitarist, was one of the verified attendees of the 100 Club Punk Special in autumn 1976, the band forming the month after this event.

At first a raucous outfit inspired by the chaotic energy of punk's first year, they quickly developed into something which as early as 1977 foreshadowed what would happen to punk rock after the main explosion. That year saw the arrival on Harvest Records of an album considered striking and influential even on release: *Pink Flag.* Newman was the instigator of much that happened in and around the band, including being the main songwriter, but the unit as a whole had much to commend it. As 1977 passed by and punk moved from being a London-centric and music paper affair to something of national significance, Wire began following sidetracks off the main punk highway, so that when the debut album was released in November it was noted for its mixture of unusual timbres and tricky song constructions. This latter aspect marked them out as something a little different. There was even a hint of prog amidst the cut-and-thrust tracks and complex structures. The music's lyrics, meanwhile, developed into something which would give Newman and the band a reputation for intellectual themes and obtuse obscurity, hardly the norm in a field of working-class angst and rage against the establishment, albeit that elitism was never part of their thematic material. Yet the economic use of instrumentation and the radical attitude to music marked them out as, if nothing else, a critical vector of the punk ethos of following an individual muse no matter what. Conventional they were not.

The album – austere, minimal, even bleak in places – was significant enough to become a classic, foreshadowing the arrival of New Wave and post-punk during the following year. The second album, *Chairs Missing,* released a few months after The Stranglers' post-punk declaration *Black & White,* developed the band's sound into something more lush, even exotic, with synthesizer additions swirling around the mix. But misunderstandings and commercial imperatives led to their record label dropping them in 1979 after a difficult third album, with a fourth album released on the Beggars Banquet record label as Newman's solo debut.

Another of the bands who were punk, yet not quite punk, was Television. As far back as 1973, this American outfit had roots, music and a reputation. Growing out of the friendship between Tom Miller, aka Verlaine, and Richard Lester Meyers, the latter soon to be unleashed upon the world as Richard Hell, the band had by 1975 found a manager and released a single on his record label. But that year saw friction between the more proficient style of the trio of Verlaine, Billy Ficca and Richard Lloyd, and Hell, whose manic presence was striking but, in the eyes of the trio, somewhat irritating. Soon enough Hell departed, meeting up with ex-New York Dolls man Johnny Thunders to form another highly significant outfit, The Heartbreakers.

The genesis of the classic Television LP *Marquee Moon* was material worked up by the band during 1976. In un-punk fashion they carefully prepared for the recording sessions, their music characterised by a punk vibe – a garage band style, as Americans called it – and more adventurous musical diversification, typified by their use of interwoven guitar parts during instrumental sections. With major label backing and positive reviews, band and album looked good, but success in their home nation did not arrive, while in Britain the album was acclaimed but lumped in with other punk sidetrack LPs. It certainly did not sound like a punk album, yet it manifested the ethic.

This was another album whose influence upon what followed belied its sound and ambition. But like Wire, the band's second album was more mellow, signifying that punk was done and dusted and post-punk was upon the music scene. And as with Wire, the band split soon after owing to internal friction and a difference in vision between artists and record label.

Richard Hell, meanwhile, had not been idle. After a stint with The Heartbreakers he formed Richard Hell and the Voidoids, a band rooted in the New York of 1976. His stage persona with Television had epitomised the raw, furious energy expressed by punks, to the extent that Verlaine and others considered him to be upstaging themselves, and even the music. By now a distinct pre-punk movement had developed in New York, a scene whose denim-clad vector The Ramones would inspire much of what happened during 1976 in London. Hell had the spiked hair and ragged clothes which characterised early punk fashion, a style which Malcolm McLaren would later claim, erroneously, to have transported to Britain after his efforts with the New York Dolls.

The music of the band was inspired by that of The Stooges and Velvet Underground, but there were plenty of other influences, not least the garage sound of the groundbreaking *Nuggets* compilation LP. Punk rock was causing waves in the music business that year, and a song of Hell's, *Blank Generation,* which he had written when in Television, was released by Television's manager Terry Ork on his own label. The success of the EP on which that song featured led to the band signing to the esteemed Sire Records label, with *Blank Generation* later being recognised and lauded as a punk classic.

The original album was created during the spring of 1977, but further amendments and elaborations permitted by record company issues led to that first incarnation being overtaken by a second, recorded at a different studio. These latter cuts dominated the final LP release, with only three of the originals being considered album-worthy. The album certainly had punk attitude. Hell considered himself, his band and his times to be part of upheavals occurring in pop and rock music generally, with the "blank" of *Blank Generation* being a metaphor for the artist creating anything their individual muse suggested. His vocals were raw and immersive, ranging from shrieks and groans to other emotion-laden utterances. Many found this style of singing too crude and piercing to take seriously, but others disagreed, and it was not long before the album took its place in the canon of early punk classics. Without doubt it had the intensity, angst and fiery fury of many punk records. Yet in its influences, guitar style and sonic delivery it deviated from the punk norm that in Britain was epitomised by The Clash, the Sex Pistols and The Damned.

Punk's lifetime lasted at most a couple of years, with only one year visible to the mainstream. But that is always the way with sudden musical eruptions. Created by constrained forces both musical and social, there is a period of formation, usually in a small locality, a period of development in which the sounds and themes arrive from the minds of their creators, and a period of mainstream visibility which, as it begins to consume itself amidst commercial imperatives, diversifies, goes dark and stale, then mutates into something different. The mid-sixties hippy revolution followed exactly the same path as that of punk. Six months after the arrival of the Summer of Love, west coast hippies and other commentators from the peace 'n' love generation were sounding the death knell of all things groovy. By the end of the year the way was set for early signs of progressive rock, a return for some, notably The Beatles, to rock 'n' roll basics, and a recognition that psychedelic music had spawned a host of subcultures all as valuable as the original movement. Punk followed the same trajectory. It exploded in London, developed in the latter half of 1976, then achieved recognition in mass media the following year. But as that year progressed, music appeared which held the seeds of diversification. Punk rock was at least as significant as the hippy movement, and at the time was a force for extraordinary change. Yet it transpired that much of that force would emerge in the sumptuous, luxuriant flourishing of innumerable sub-genres after the explosion, musical forms which laid the foundation for the music business as we know it today: the importance of indie labels, the following of a muse regardless of convention, and the significance of music for society in general. Without punk there would most likely have been no ska revival and no 2 Tone Records, amongst many other outcrops. Britain has always prided itself on the quality, style and originality of its music, which is ironic given the almost complete lack of support received from established institutions, most of which are all too keen to bathe in reflected glory. Punk rock, for all that it formed from an American movement with that name, acquired in Britain a unique form, intensity and social manifestation the like of which will never be seen again.

Punk did diversify, and quickly, giving rise to new forms which would themselves grow, mutate and gain recognition. In doing so, it lost its roots; an inevitable process. A second generation of punk bands did emerge, but they often inhabited a different sound-world to their forebears: GBH, The Exploited, and Crass. But from the end of the 1950s punk was part of a four-decade sweep of musical development which would characterise two generations of young people, as well as delighting them, giving them identity, powering their drive to freedom and allowing them free expression. All four of those qualities were critical to young people, not least the punks. They needed to be delighted, especially after the horrors of war and the interminable grey days of post-war gloom; they had to find new identities in a country developing with speed into a new kind of nation, social changes which left them confused and in a rut; they needed to free themselves from political restraints, the majority of which were imposed upon them by an elitist, narcissistic class of individuals; and they wanted free expression – to tell their own stories, to find their way amidst the flak of economic stagnation and mismanagement, to become who they could be.

Punk was the fuel for so many of those stories. For the lucky few, it powered their personal and musical development, at first in the capital city, then in the country at large. For those who saw punk at a distance, it became an inspiration. As it diversified it brought into focus a new, expansive horizon, before which great new musicians and amazing new bands stood, hands at their brows, surveying the revealed view. As the iconic figures of punk turned to other forms – John Lydon to Public Image Limited, the Damned to a new breed of gothic rock, The Clash to reggae and other world music forms, Siouxsie to her own brand of goth – the movement itself died, its body raked over, consumed then digested by a multitude of other genres.

The corpus of punk in LP format remained for all to witness and enjoy, and, like all deaths after a life well lived, punk's afterlife consisted of ripple after ripple and wave after wave through rock music. The oft-repeated refrain *'Punk's Not Dead'* is both actually and metaphorically true. Punk is not dead because bands following the original style continue to make great music. But punk is also not dead for the same reason Thomas Paine is not dead. His work lives on.

Chapter 26

The Brutal, Dark Denouement

Real name: Simon John Ritchie. Stage name: Sid Vicious. He could not play any instrument competently, but he was an ardent follower of the Sex Pistols and he wanted to get on stage. In due course he took up bass as his best option under the circumstances.

Former Rainbow Theatre front of house man Hal Harries remembered him from when Vicious and the other three members of the Pistols visited the venue in Finsbury Park: "Sid was crazy, out of control." Vicious embodied the self-destructive element of punk, the nihilistic ideal that brought down everything, including himself. But he manifested that ideal, rather than intellectualising about it.

His home life and upbringing through the late 1950s into the 1960s was chaotic and dangerous. He lacked either a father or a step-father, and his mother Anne succumbed to heroin, becoming an addict by the time Vicious, then calling himself John Beverley, was sixteen and at school. That year, at Kingsway College of Further Education, he met fellow student John Lydon, and along with two of Lydon's friends, John Grey and John Wardle (later to become Public Image Limited's brilliant bassist Jah Wobble), they were collectively known as the Four Johns. Soon the quartet had given up on school and were squatting in a variety of squalid locations.

By 1975 and the first stirrings of punk on the streets of London, Vicious along with others could be found at the SEX shop on the King's Road in Chelsea, where, drifting from poorly played instrument to poorly played instrument, he became known as a member of the nascent movement. He knew Chrissie Hynde, NME journalist and occasional Pistols guitarist Nick Kent, Viv Albertine and Keith Levene. By autumn 1976 he was sufficiently known to play drums at the 100 Club Punk Special as part of the debut appearance by Siouxsie and the Banshees. However, the following day, pissed and high on speed, he threw the notorious beer glass that would result in a girl in the audience losing sight in one eye. Taken to Ashford Remand Centre under arrest, he was visited by Albertine accompanied by Vivienne Westwood.

In February 1977, following growing antagonism between Glen Matlock and John Lydon, Matlock departed the Sex Pistols. But there was more to it than just tension between young men. Malcolm McLaren followed a management style that created the maximum amount of publicity-worthy chaos, and if that meant fracturing the band, so be it. Matlock supposedly liked The Beatles – a sin amongst punks, for all that Lydon was a fan of progressive heroes Van Der Graaf Generator. But there was more to it even than that. Vicious manifested the moody, nihilistic aspect of punk, that bleak, black anger running through its veins. Resentment was visible on his face, could be heard in his voice and experienced through his actions. McLaren had observed all this for months, and knew Vicious would make the Sex Pistols a more newsworthy entity than they were already. The split was engineered so that Vicious could arrive, bass guitar in tow. He would stand beside Johnny Rotten and Steve Jones at front of stage.

And he had always been an obsessed fan of the Pistols. Encouraged by McLaren and his associates to play to his worst side, he became the blackest sheep among that dark flock, epitomising their nihilism; the heedless, chaotic figurehead of a foul-mouthed squad. But he loved that. He cared nothing for consequences.

His debut that April at the Screen On The Green became a cameo in Don Letts' film *The Punk Rock Movie.* Thus would the beginning of the end both of the Sex Pistols and punk be immortalised.

Yet even as the band's permanent bassist he was often absent. His lack of musicality meant that when the time came to record *Never Mind The Bollocks, Here's The Sex Pistols* his contributions were so poor Steve Jones had to assume bass duties. In fact, the track *Bodies* did have a Sid Vicious bass part for a while, but even that was replaced when it came to preparing the LP for release. As rehearsals arrived Vicious was to be found in hospital with hepatitis following his wide-ranging drug use. The newsworthy behaviour McLaren craved was present and plentiful, but its chaotic aspect was proving difficult to work with. Yet he appeared on stage just enough to consolidate his position in the band and his status as a crucial punk figure.

One of the other figures of the SEX crowd was drug addict and dealer Nancy Spungen, an American living in London whose unsavoury past recommended itself to those inhabiting the underbelly of the punk movement. Vicious became her ideal, and she his. Their chaotic, unstable lives, addictions and violent obsessions (both were physically abusive) made them perfect for one another. Yet some amongst the band and their cohort were less than pleased with this relationship, and there were rumblings of discontent, even at the very top. Malcolm McLaren later claimed he tried to have Spungen bundled onto a plane back to America.

As it happened, America would be the location for the grim and brutal end of the Sid Vicious story. The American tour dates of January 1978 were McLaren's ideal of chaos, with Vicious alternately attacking himself and members of the audience; himself with a razor blade, the audience with insults and his bass. By the time of the final gig in San Francisco, things were so bad there were stories that his bass was not even plugged in. That, ironically, proved to be incorrect. But what was true was that the Sex Pistols were over. It was soon discovered that Lydon had jumped ship – the voice of punk silencing himself.

Warner Brothers, the band's American record label, had insisted as part of the tour arrangements that Vicious give up heroin and use methadone instead. On board a plane from San Francisco to New York he fell into an alcohol and methadone coma, from which he surfaced later, in hospital. There, he was told in no uncertain terms that his life was on the line if he did not give up alcohol.

Alongside Spungen, Vicious attended filming in Paris for Julien Temple's documentary *The Great Rock 'N' Roll Swindle,* but as ever he was a slave to drugs, and filming was sporadic. Yet Temple managed to film him performing a trio of cover versions, which, with the Pistols no longer an operational unit, became potential solo songs. These were: *My Way,* the Frank Sinatra classic, and the rock 'n' roll standards *C'mon Everybody* and *Something Else.* By now the co-dependent relationship between him and Spungen was becoming dangerous to both, with Spungen cutting herself in revenge for perceived slights. By summer, the pair were back in London. There, Vicious met Glen Matlock, the latter playing in his new outfit Rich Kids. Matlock suggested Vicious join him for a gig, which duly took place at Camden's Electric Ballroom in August. For this event, Vicious himself was the vocalist, Spungen behind him on backing vocals, albeit inaudible because of her inability to sing.

This combination of Vicious and Spungen on stage then returned to America, where Spungen, exploiting her contacts, put together a motley group of musicians to act as Vicious' band. As before, the relationship between front man and audience was fractious, with Vicious being both insulting and also not much of a singer. These events were recorded, appearing in due course as the LP *Sid Sings.*

By now, even Spungen was becoming aware that her and Vicious' drug habits were leading to potentially life-changing illness. A spiral of hospitals and trauma lay before them both. Reports began to drift among the inner circle that money was required for detoxification programmes, which would not be cheap.

The end of the road was in sight.

During a drug-fuelled party in a hotel room on 11 October, events murky at the time and debated by all – including by Malcolm McLaren – led to the death of Nancy Spungen from a knife wound to the abdomen. Vicious gave rambling, inconsistent accounts of the events of that night, leading to his arrest for second degree murder. He alternately confessed to the stabbing, to seeing Spungen fall upon the knife, and to remembering nothing at all. McLaren and Vicious' mother tried to find the best lawyer for the defence, and at length Vicious was released on bail, Richard Branson stumping up the costs. But by now Vicious was in a dangerous mental state, cutting himself and behaving with chaotic disregard for his own safety. An official assessment of the time stated that he should not be left on his own, for fear of suicide or accidental, self-inflicted injury. Various hospital visits followed, but on 26 November he was taken back to the Chelsea Hotel, where he and Spungen had stayed. Yet he was still active and mentally alert. In an interview two days later he spoke about Spungen, rambling on about her fate as he, and apparently she, saw it. McLaren meanwhile, in one of his most callous acts, announced that the Sex Pistols would reunite in order to fund Vicious' legal costs.

Out and about in New York, Vicious continued to instigate violent events, leading to his arrest for assault and then enforced detoxification at the Rikers Island correctional institute. On 18 January he appeared in court, but the presiding judge reduced his bail and weakened its conditions. Vicious' mother was now in America, visiting her son at Rikers Island and involving herself with the defence. But when Vicious was released from the correctional institute at the beginning of February, he at once began scoring drugs. That night he died from an overdose. Inevitably, accounts of the reason for his death varied.

He was born into a dysfunctional world, yet did not have even a dysfunctional family. Effectively, he had no family. For all that his mother supported and defended him when his life began its death spiral, Vicious' mind was rootless and isolated, drawing on the cultural zeitgeist of the time and his own luck in meeting Lydon and the rest of the gang in order to gain some kind of identity. He had no plan for life, unless the various suicide notes and dark letters discovered and presented later hold any personal truths. He was the self-destructive type. He cared nothing for consequences. He wanted to be seen on stage with the Sex Pistols, he wanted to be visible there, adored, feared, hated. In fact it did not matter what emotions he engendered in others; what mattered was the attention and the kudos. It was his prime motivation, though he was never aware of it. His cruelty and aggression were those of the typical boy. His reckless, full-tilt life was that of the typical teenager. Although some who knew him as a friend observed a few redeeming qualities, in the main he was violent, out of control and heedless of the consequences of his actions. He was foul-mouthed and full of antagonism. He was vicious.

Punk was home to a full range of characters. It had its creative giants, it had its visionaries, it had its philosophers. It was a rainbow movement, albeit rather a monochrome one, founded on injustice, fuelled by anger, and given credence by Britain's fertile music scene. For every Hugh Cornwell, Mark Perry and Joe Strummer there was a lesser version of Simon John Ritchie, balancing out creative fire with suffocating blankets of hopeless, useless nihilism. Vicious was the leader of that pack. And he wanted to be there, sneering with curled lip, insulting his audience, destroying, destroying, destroying. Punk, after all, was at heart a movement containing all human life; exactly as would be expected. It had moments of musical brilliance and it had moments of bleak abandon. It had its leaders and its followers.

It had creators and destroyers. Lydon, Matlock, Jones and Cook were creators. Vicious was the destroyer. They manifested their grim, working class lives, but with a wit and insight that flecked what stood around them with light. Vicious manifested a traumatised childhood, painting that black background with bloodied splashes of grey. The lock and chain that as Sid Vicious he wore around his neck came from deep in his past, the chain his lack of insight, the padlock the heroin he needed to bury the agony of his injurious childhood.

Chapter 27

The Legacy

In the end, what did it all add up to? Is there a legacy? *Can* there be a legacy from something so explosive, or was punk akin to a scorched earth policy, erasing the past in favour of a brand new nihilistic future, which remains unseen because it never arrived?

It is true that punk was punk *rock,* a musical form. Music being one way human beings express feelings and emotions in a cultural setting, punk was created from notes, chords and rhythms, with lyrics placed on top. Punk was three-minute songs: *God Save The Queen.* Punk was forty-minute albums: *The Stranglers IV, Rattus Norvegicus.* Punk was gigs: the 100 Club Punk Special. Punk was radio play: the John Peel sessions. Punk was music on film: *The Punk Rock Movie.*

The British pride themselves on the depth and breadth of their pop and rock music tradition. The Beatles were British, as are Elton John, Led Zeppelin, Pink Floyd and other multi-platinum-selling behemoths. In 1967, British culture ruled the musical world, challenged only by what had happened months before on America's West Coast. Just nine years separated the Summer of Love and the punk explosion. Yet that cultural eyeblink in time stands between the hippy-dippy frolics of Syd Barrett's Pink Floyd, lounging in dappled sunlight beside the River Cam, and the screaming, ferocious, blood and phlegm-spattered urgency of the Pistols' *Anarchy In The U.K.,* with Johnny Rotten ordering his gobsmacked audience to get off their arses. Those nine years seem far too short a time for such a transformation to take place.

It would seem that punk rock was a *reaction* to something. That can be generally agreed. It was a reaction to several stultifying conditions of British society which coalesced by accident in the first half of the 1970s. Those conditions were political, social and musical. The first set of conditions originated in the hidebound two party system that Britain has never had the insight or courage to abandon, and which led to, for instance, safe Conservative seats in rural constituencies being held since Victorian times. The next set of conditions were sourced in a rigid, elitist, self-absorbed hierarchy based on class – one of the strictest such systems in the world. It has been observed that the peculiarly British sense of humour, which emanates from a sensitivity to all things absurd, is sourced in this debilitating class system and the farcical individuals at the summit. The third set of conditions was musical: an often lazy and smug reliance on self-selecting networks and other forms of privilege which gifted the nation progressive rock as well as glam. To be fair, there were many glints of gold in prog rock. Few would argue with the thrilling melodiousness of Pink Floyd's *Echoes,* or the visionary urgency of Yes' masterpiece *The Gates Of Delerium.* Very few would argue that *Phaedra* and *Rubycon* by Tangerine Dream were not groundbreaking, or that *Stairway To Heaven,* for years the pinnacle of John Peel's Festive 50, was not a remarkable song. But against those must be placed the dull, often trite meanderings of lesser groups, who also ran. There was gold in glam too, notably that provided for a short period by David Bowie. All this, then, was the backdrop to what punks loathed. It was the warp and weft of their country, against which they reacted. Punk was kickback; and not before time.

But it was more than that.

Human beings are distinguishable from animals because of their use of a mental model of reality, rather than relying on instinct. This results in a number of unique characteristics, including the fact that a human life must be actively *lived.* No human being, unless profoundly ill or trapped in some way, can allow life to live *them*, as happens with animals. This leads to various consequences, including an ethical sense, a desire for explanation and meaning – merged into storytelling – and an urgent need to find a place in life, alongside purpose or direction. These are all attributes of typical individuals wherever they might live and from whatever epoch. Human beings, then, are active in the world, seeking meaning, aligning themselves with ethical positions or standards. They are *doers.* They make things, achieve things, change things.

The defining years for punk were 1976-77. The central characters of the explosion were various and notable, coming from a variety of backgrounds.

There was Johnny Rotten, Rat Scabies, Siouxsie Sioux, Hugh Cornwell, Poly Styrene and Pete Shelley – all of them unforgettable. Though each differed in their outlook and style, all of these remarkable individuals were on a mission to *act* in the world, to bring their musical or lyrical vision to others for the sake either of better music or, perhaps, a better country. *Anarchy In The U.K.* is an ethical statement reacting against the absurd, narcissistic, decaying heartland of the British establishment. *God Save The Queen* is a profound ethical statement exposing what John Lydon saw as ivory-tower individuals living in a number of large and luxurious buildings across a nation riven by inequality. Beneath their hats of gold, those individuals declaimed to the British commoners arranged at their feet, their fantasy world one in which they "served," and the proles were grateful for it.

That perverse twisting of the truth was more than apparent to Lydon as he wrote one of his greatest songs. A human being of intelligence and learning, he felt the need to *act.* He sensed the great weight of the class-based hierarchy above him, he sensed its lack of relevance and meaning to him, and he sensed its callous disregard for those swathes of society it cared nothing about, though it professed to. He knew all this because *he* lived the truth. It was *his* political reality, his social reality, his cultural reality. His musical reality was made plain by the legend on that famous T shirt: *I Hate Pink Floyd.* That was not just something he wanted to react against, it was something he wished to *articulate.* He wanted to live an active life by speaking truth to power, by exposing unjust social circumstances, by pointing out and mocking the comical features of prog rock, in which that genre was often wrapped, immune to the world, like the emperor's new clothes if those garments could be made of invisible cotton wool. Lydon was not going to sit back and consume Pepsi and crisps, or buy a flash red car, or acquire a better job to get one over his peers and make himself feel better. Those options were *dead* options. They were *passive.* If he walked that path his mind would die, and then his body.

Politicians who make lists of fundamental human needs usually apply themselves to physical needs: food and water, warmth and secure housing, transport and a basic income. They either forget or simply have not realised that this is only half the list. Just as important are psychological needs, and those needs include artistic expression. Such list-makers do not realise or cannot be bothered to mention that if a human being does not have water and food their body dies, but if a human being does not have creative expression and individual or community purpose their mind dies, regardless of how well fed they are. Both are forms of death.

This is the brutaltruth of Thatcher's undying (and often misquoted) epigram: *there is no such thing as society, only individual men and women and their families.* In that sentence, Thatcher enunciated a novel variation on the established British way, which most equate with conservatism and Conservatism. Yet the callousness which most critics of Thatcher assume is there, but which some say is not, really *is* there. What she meant was that she thought social institutions and systems were interdependent and arose "naturally." She presumed the existence of certain social norms, but, critically, failed to realise that such norms said everything about her and her narcissistic view and nothing about human society. She simply assumed she was correct about everything. She was, therefore, drawn to the unchanging – that is, conservative – elements of British society, for which tradition, history, empire and much more are core concepts.

John Lydon felt upon his shoulders the rigid, prejudiced, elitist weight of that conservatism, just as he might feel the weight of a flash red car. It ground him into the streets of London. It was relentless and remorseless, trying to turn him into a passive consumer, hypnotised by the neon lights of advertising, addicted to fat and to salt and to sugar. It denied him almost every form of creative expression. It told him he was the child of lesser immigrants. It spoke to him of tedium and the dead hand of inequality. It offered neither opportunity nor hope.

Lydon, however, had one ace up his sleeve. It was the ace all human beings have, if only they can find the insight to see it. That ace was the card of *action.*

Very few personal, community or social circumstances are so horrific or domineering nothing can be achieved by action. In wartime, such circumstances do exist, but 1976 was not one of those times. They also exist within authoritarian state systems such as the ones controlling the Russian and Chinese peoples. Britain in 1976 was pretty bad, but it was at least a nation of mostly free speech with a democratic system which, though rigged and unjust, did offer an occasional alternative to "the natural party of power in Britain."

Punk – its first, shaky stirrings – was something that arose naturally, from the streets, in response to the circumstances of the time. That early, it was unaware of its own importance; a movement of comparative innocence. Only later did it become aware of itself as a social force, something which was being observed by individuals of the establishment, in the music biz, and elsewhere. In those early days, Lydon simply acted as his motives dictated. The punk label had yet to be invented.

It is true that Lydon was lucky. What if he had been wearing a T shirt emblazoned with *I Like Iggy Pop?* That somehow is not so empowering, not so radical, nor half as witty as the legend on the real T shirt. What if he had been wearing one of Vivienne Westwood's cobweb sweaters over his T shirt? Perhaps then he might not have been able to act in the way he did; he might never have been spotted. There would possibly have been no Sex Pistols, at least not in the way they are known today, and Britain would have been diminished as a result. All these possibilities are matters of chance. But being active means *using* your chances when they turn up. Luck is random, but individuals can skew the odds against them by following every path and lead, should they so desire – should they *feel* the need. Some people are just too numb even to do that. Lydon could have tucked into a burger and drunk a bottle of lager, but he did not. He sensed an opportunity. He actively lived his life. He noticed things. He had purpose, forged in the bitter circumstances of his young life, alive with intelligence, and fuelled by the iniquities in plain view all around him. He became Johnny Rotten, sang for the Sex Pistols, and the rest is history.

Punk rock had a manifesto, and it could be summed up as D.I.Y. *Do it yourself.* That manifesto was a cry to all those who resented the weight of oppression, tedium and injustice which characterised Britain in the 1970s. D.I.Y. was not just a shout out to proto-punks, nor a rallying cry to prog-hating musicians, it was a cry to human beings, designed to appeal to their fundamental psychological needs. It said: *you live in an elitist, unjust, rigged, stultifying country, but if you act now you could change that. The odds are against you, but if you do not act you are bound to fail, whereas if you do act you might fail. The choice is yours.*

Facing this, and inspired in the main by the Sex Pistols, dozens of characters now admired, adored and respected saw inside their sleeves the great ace in the playing card pack of life. Pete Shelley and Howard Devoto were two, transporting the punk message with almost indecent haste to Manchester. Siouxsie and Poly Styrene were two more, inspiring young women. But soon there were innumerable such characters across the nation, all hearing the call to their essential human nature, that, if they made an effort, organised themselves and actively lived their lives, they could not only make a different to their own wellbeing they could perhaps influence the wellbeing of the nation. Thus it was that punk was not just a musical and cultural explosion, it was a *human* explosion. It dazzled young people, shocked them, then inspired them, shaking them out of the paralysis induced in them with deliberate malice by established British systems. Using their chosen vehicles of bands and music, they exposed, opposed and damaged those systems. Punk was a working-class, anti-establishment movement, but it was a movement attractive and available to all oppressed groups, including women, people of colour, and immigrants. It spoke to *everybody* feeling the dead weight of conservatism, of prejudiced social institutions, and of a self-serving elite.

"Get off your arse!" meant *wake up*.

And this is why punk *does* have a legacy. Moreover, that legacy is in 2024 more important than ever. The legacy has in fact become universal.

In 2024, Britain faces a corporate economic landscape of worsening inequality, obscene injustice and never-ending commercial aggrandisement. The British people exist in the main to nourish and grow those corporations. The masses are corporate food, live as their underlings, and act as their experimental subjects, not least online. It is no accident that corporations jumped onto the internet bandwagon as soon as they realised what potential it offered them, including the option of using psychological techniques which in any theatre other than commerce would be deemed not only illegal but inhumane too. The internet could strip humanity from its own brains. It could make animals of us, not merely passive, like the slack-jawed consumers of 1970s television advertisements, but operating on some trite, spartan, alienated version of instinct – human animals.

Punk attitude would be of great benefit in such times. The irony is that the days of local, geographically limited cultural scenes and movements are long gone. The internet globalises human beings so that they all live in the same vast, rigged and unfathomable level playing field. No scene will emerge from a shop, even if it is emblazoned with the word SEX. No movement will spring from the streets of Cardiff, Liverpool, or even London.

But society today needs punk. It needs that passion for D.I.Y. It needs people of all ages to wake up and realise they are being forced to live in a cell, a rather small cell, whose four walls are built from the online world, rapacious commerce, the fragmentation of society, and a host of false meanings promulgated by multinational corporations. The floor of such cells are made from shopping, the roof from lies. Food is pushed through the door by politicians. But to escape incarceration a prisoner only has to *see* their cell. They have to wake up, see truth rather than corporate and political fiction, then *Do It Themselves.* They have to break out by finding an active life, by creating meaning, even if that meaning is soaked in their own hard or tragic circumstances. This was the fundamental hope of punk, that from difficult, poverty-stricken, hopeless and downtrodden lives meaning could be found, meaning that makes life worth living, for all that such meaning was clothed in the tropes of the working class, was fuelled by rage, and sounded to many ears discordant. What mattered was that punk was *meaning* for young people in those years of the 1970s – their *own* meaning. It spoke to the human condition that they all contained. They owned punk because they designed it.

Nor was any particular talent required. When Siouxsie Sioux asked Malcolm McLaren if she could sing at the 100 Club Punk Special, she had no idea what she might offer the audience. Though she had talent and would become extraordinary in later years, she was in 1976 nascent, unformed, with only her attitude to motivate her. Yet it was that attitude, emerging from the recesses of her subconscious, which made her take herself into her hands and *do* something with life. Punk both inspired her and articulated her desire to live.

Punk is polemic. And that is okay. Polemic is valuable because it is thought and speech fuelled by emotion. Too often emotion supposedly “fogs” the brain and “confuses” clear thought, but the truth is different. Moreover, in

Britain, the rules about being emotional are particularly harsh and absurd, especially for men. Emotion, including anger, is all about *value.* Without value human beings would lead lives of one quality: beige, bland, antiseptic. Punk was not just angry, it was angry about something *worth* being angry about. It was angry because the social systems it arose from were, and still are, inhumane. Those systems were designed for elites, for corporations, and for a political system just about fit for the eighteenth century. That was something worth feeling rage about. Punk articulated that anger with vibrancy and passion.

True, in some instances punk became nihilistic – the fundamentalist branch of the movement. But actually, quite a few punk musicians were uneasy with that nihilism, or even spoke against it. Regardless of that, however, their rage was justified. The anger just had to come out, because that is the point of emotions – they *have* to be experienced because the knowledge they convey must never be missed.

Such was the case in 1976 in Britain.

The presumption amongst the young is that music can change society; that *musicians* can change society. But is that a realistic view?

Change in society can come about by accident or by design. In the latter case it is more often due to communities of people than individuals. Instances of individuals bringing about significant social change are rare. Yet change brought about by single musicians dominates the conversation, including the one in this book. Think of John Lydon, frequently mentioned here.

Through luck or design, some individuals, like him, acquire potential for change beyond the norm. We can all have an effect on our families or peer groups, and some of us, either by virtue of work or by being born in privileged circumstances, can bring about considerable change locally – even nationally. Some individuals however can bring about change by virtue of the voice they acquire. In this instance it is not that they themselves, by virtue of specific actions, cause social change, rather that merely by being alive and being themselves they act as a catalyst for mass social change. That type of social change is at least as potent as that brought about by the French Revolution or by Tony Blair. It is the force of social change created by inspiration.

When historians of music think about John Lydon, they often think about the man's influence on the huge range of young people who saw him and the Sex Pistols during 1976 and 1977. They think about how, through his intense, confrontational manner, through his challenging lyrics, and through his take-no-prisoners interviewing style on television and radio, Lydon was able to galvanise a whole section of society into mass action. To do this, he had to show them the nature of their prison, which he himself felt to a painful degree. The chances of his own circumstances – the existence of The Ramones and their arrival in London, living in the capital city, being born in 1956 – meant that he fell by accident into a position which he could use to change society. And he *wanted* to do that. It was not that he himself, an individual man, nor even as a man in a group of restless youths, was able through his own efforts to bring about a fairer, more just society. He did not fight for that with a sword or a revolver. Rather, through charisma, intelligence and insight, and because he understood that his own suffering was shared by innumerable others of his age and social class, he was able to galvanise them into the sort of action which did change their lives, and thus society. He was a *vector* of social change.

Too often people think social change must be brought about by force, by the wielding of power, or by influence through the usual channels: politics, religion. Too often it is thought that social change must come only from politics, or preaching, or even via military action. Those are certainly some options. But how much more profound and more lasting is the social change brought about by Lydon speaking truth not only to power but to his own contemporaries – hundreds of thousands of them. His influence continues today. His lyrics, and the music of the Sex Pistols continue today. 1976 really *was* a turning point in Britain, and that should never be forgotten. Punk was critical to the progress of the British nation from benighted, miserable post-war austerity to the flash and thrill of punk rock.

True, Lydon does seem to have backed himself into a corner in recent years, with his support for Brexit and various unmentionable American politicians. But this is not difficult to understand. During his young life he defined himself as somebody in opposition to something else, with that something else being the leviathan of the British establishment. He considered himself an outsider. Deep in his subconscious he feels like a perpetual outsider. Now, having moved away from the country which never accepted him as he truly was, he sees the vast bloc of political and social opinion weighing against the Right and other purveyors of conservatism and he defines himself as being opposed to *that.* It does not matter what the content of the opinions or views are. The content is immaterial. What matters is that he defines himself against the larger bloc. He saw this new bloc of opinion hove into view – a new online establishment, as it were – and he felt the urge to oppose it. This act of opposition, generating opprobrium just as it did in 1976, satisfies his need to feel like an outsider fighting for something. In his youth, he fought the establishment bloc. Now, he fights the online establishment bloc – the liberals, the rational, the centre ground. He *must* fight, must oppose, must position himself in a location which brings the ire, astonishment and disgust of others. And such has he done.

Lydon's recent behaviour is not an enigma at odds with his rebellious past. Indeed, he has acted true to type. This is because he feels the tides of social affairs more deeply than most, and therefore feels the need to ride them, to actualise them and to explain them. As most people who came into his orbit observed, he was smart. But he was not only smart, he was sensitive and a thinker. This was to the advantage of himself, and, as it turned out, the British nation. His appearance in society at large however was pure chance. But because he was smart and sensitive and a thinker, *and* an opportunist, he inspired social change far beyond the norm for one of his upbringing and social class. He was lucky. Everyone is who has been touched by his character. Britain is lucky that he manifested that great credo of punk: do it yourself, do it now, be *active.* Lydon was no passive citizen. He was a doer. That inspired thousands upon thousands of others to be doers also, to their great advantage.

But that tide of punk action was not just to the advantage of everyone who was part of it. Being a punk in 1976 meant reducing the chances of going insane through boredom, passivity and hopelessness. For the majority of young people in 1976, the prison confining them was difficult to see. Lydon exposed the nature of the cell walls surrounding them.

Some people horrified by Lydon's manner, for instance when he appeared on television – part pugnacious, part sullen, part sweary – thought him mentally diminished, or, if not that, socially compromised in some way.

Some people thought him disgusting, outrageous, appalling, dangerous, frightening. Theirs was an entirely negative reaction. Yet the truth was different. Through his actions, Lydon was defining himself as an *artist,* then communicating that fact. He was psychologically authenticating himself by the act of making art; music, in his case, alongside a small band of contemporaries. Far from being compromised or diminished, or espousing the values of revolution because of some inner lack, he was comporting himself as a healthy individual. He was manifesting his sanity. It was in fact the cohorts of tradition, watching television or reading their newspapers in passive mode, eating their dinners and making their money, not noticing the world as it collapsed around their ears, not bothering to struggle against the forces suppressing them, not aware of the weight of the chains confining them, who were mentally compromised. They were the ones into whom false needs were inculcated by corporations, politicians and economic snake-oil salesmen. They were the ill ones, the spoiled, the wasted, the empty. They were heading towards insanity. It was Lydon who was the exemplar of sanity, observing the world, feeling it, then acting as a consequence of those feelings. All those complaining about his manner, his appearance, his bad language and his values were the mentally unhealthy ones. *They* lived in darkness. He, in comparison, was a beacon of light.

Chapter 28

Post

It was a cold, snowy day in England at the end of 1977. The nation stumbled towards Christmas, battered by punk, politically riven and uneasy, waiting for Christmas Eve and the beginning of a proper break.

At Bear Shank Lodge, a house owned by photographer Ruan O'Lochlainn, there was nobody about. Built near Oundle in the middle of the Northamptonshire countryside, the place and its surrounds were deserted, its eerie aura intensified by the chilly weather. Snow carpeted the ground and the wind felt freezing. To this place came The Stranglers, buoyed by their success during the year, but facing the new year with no material and high expectations, not least from their record company. The quartet realised they would have to write with intent, to order, composing rather than allowing songs to naturally appear, and all within a limited time frame. It was not going to be easy.

There was a rehearsal room inside the house, but with the nearest human beings some distance away the band could write and play whenever they wished to – noise was not going to be a problem. Billy Bragg would visit on occasion, as did Lora Logic. Apart from that, the place remained untroubled by visitors.

In due course Jet Black, Hugh Cornwell and Dave Greenfield departed for the Christmas break, leaving Jean-Jacques Burnel to enjoy the solitude and bitter weather.

The songs the band wrote were intense, often futuristic, and musically adventurous. A desire to transcend punk limitations fuelled their writing, marked in particular by the acquisition of new synthesizers, which Greenfield played with lugubrious style. The Hohner Cembalet and Hammond organ were still part of his set up, but now a new sound world had arrived, travelling on the wings of squelchy solos and deep, resonant bass frequencies. All four wanted to escape the fashions and tribal loyalties of punk, to wear black and expand their musical horizons; to travel in sound, to explore a new landscape, to blaze new trails. That landscape would in due course be named post-punk.

Black And White turned out to be the band's masterpiece. Today, in 2024, it *still* sounds futuristic. The first post-punk album, it led the way into what looked like a dystopian future, its music powered by the weird atmosphere of the house and the woozy feeling in each of the musicians that atmosphere generated. There were songs about tanks and travel, songs about the mysteries of time, of Sweden, of robots: Versatran Series F. *Toiler On The Sea,* ending the LP's white side and an acknowledged classic, spoke of mysterious journeys, flocks of seagulls, and the dark miasma surrounding interpersonal relationships. The black side spoke of political strife and martial law, weird feelings of paranoia, the nature of government and political convention, Yukio Mishima, shadows and the dark precipitation of nuclear fallout… do you have enough time?

Punk was over. The Stranglers were mutating into a stark new form, O'Lochlainn's photograph for the LP's front cover showing them in monochrome, Cornwell with his head bowed, Burnel crouching, almost foetal, Greenfield with a strange hand. Only Jet Black, the foreground figure, looked relatively normal. It was a great photograph for an exceptional album. Post-punk had arrived.

The heat and drought of 1976 was long gone. Memories of the riots, tirades and fury of 1977 were already fading. In Britain's music scene, new shoots were emerging, but they were strange and as yet half-formed, one part guitars, one part synthesizers, one part industrial, one part glitzy. New Wave was a lighter, brighter companion to post-punk, the latter carrying some of the minimal intensity of punk through its novel soundscapes. Fans could dance to a lot of New Wave songs; no pogoing or gobbing. Punk had smashed prog and injured pop, but New Wave managed to heal wounds. Prog would change, though slowly. New Wave was a catch-all for a return to normality, albeit with a backward glance at the wreckage left by the punk explosion.

Punk was done, but not dead. Its essential mantras lived on.

Do It Yourself. Do It Now.

Independence and action.

Those messages should never fade.

Bibliography & Resources

Czezowski, Andrew & Carrington, Susan, *The Roxy,* Carrczez Publishing Ltd, *2017*
Drury, Jim & Cornwell, Hugh, *The Stranglers Song By Song,* Bobcat Publishing, *2011*
Wall, Mick, *John Peel,* Orion, *2004*

Websites
Sex Pistols
www.sexpistolsofficial.com

Sex Pistols *So It Goes* video
https://youtu.be/VhfcX9VQcMs?si=JddCgom89h5To1nj

Dave Goodman
www.discogs.com/es/artist/250494-Dave-Goodman

New Rose
https://amp.theguardian.com/music/2018/how-we-made-the-damned-new-rose

Rat Scabies interviewed by Piccadilly Radio, Manchester: audio
https://youtu.be/S0qqZAtvk5E?si=QHeUjXL-s1hMzNCL

The Bill Grundy Sex Pistols interview video
https://youtu.be/sraHAz8nqRQ?si=IEoM-8l0fbPzIals

Sniffin' Glue fanzine
https://sniffinglue.co.uk

The Anarchy Tour
www.bbc.co.uk/news/uk-england-norfolk-38165091.amp

The Maniacs
https://www.punk77.co.uk/groups/maniacs.htm

Eater
https://www.punk77.co.uk/groups/eater.htm

The 100 Club
https://www.the100club.co.uk/history/

100 Club Punk Special
http://www.philjens.plus.com/pistols/pistols/100club_memories.htm
https://faroutmagazine.co.uk/the-birth-of-punk-45-years-on-from-100-club-punk-special/
https://punkgirldiaries.com/100-club-punk-festival-20th-september-1976/amp/

The Roxy Club: Andrew Czezowski & Susan Carrington
https://roxyclub.co.uk/

The Damned *New Rose* video
https://youtu.be/TUxFQ5QBiYk?si=-foGFWhT2p2xLd4e

The Stranglers *No More Heroes* video
https://youtu.be/2tfy8f9lDD0?si=lXha-sL2YqDJeHK5

Sex Pistols US Tour 1978
https://faroutmagazine.co.uk/what-did-the-sex-pistols-play-at-their-final-concert/

John Peel Fandom wiki: Sessions
https://peel.fandom.com/wiki/Slits
https://peel.fandom.com/wiki/Damned
https://peel.fandom.com/wiki/Clash
https://peel.fandom.com/wiki/Sex_Pistols

God Save The Queen Thames riverboat trip
https://amp.theguardian.com/music/2012/may/29/sex-pistols-jubilee-boat-trip
https://faroutmagazine.co.uk/timeline-the-sex-pistols-crashed-the-silver-jubilee/
https://amp.theguardian.com/music/2012/apr/29/sex-pistols-queen-jubilee-boat

Never Mind The Bollocks court case
https://exchange.nottingham.ac.uk/blog/the-professor-and-the-punks/

Jenny Runacre
www.jennyrunacre.co.uk/the-making-of-jubilee

Jubilee
https://m.imdb.com/title/tt0076240